The Spirit of Promise

Donald Macleod

Christian Focus Publications

Published by
Christian Focus Publications
Geanies House,
Fearn, Tain,
Ross-shire IV20 1TW
Scotland

© 1986 Christian Focus Publications

ISBN 0 906731 48 8

Typeset in Scotland by John G. Eccles Printers Ltd, Inverness
Printed in England by Cox & Wyman

Contents

Introduction

The various chapters of this book first appeared as editorials in *The Monthly Record of the Free Church of Scotland*. The questions they deal with, however, are likely to be with us for some time. Indeed, the publication of Dr Lloyd-Jones' *Joy Unspeakable* will ensure that controversy as to the nature of Spirit baptism will continue to simmer in the Reformed churches.

It would be arrogant to suggest that the original articles attracted much attention but there has been at least sufficient reaction to justify a few words of explanation and clarification.

Man of Straw

The most fundamental objection, probably, has been that these articles are tilting at a man of straw. There is no such Christian as the writer envisages. This is true to the extent that no single Christian holds all the views discussed here. For example, those who believe that Spirit baptism is a subsequent experience do not necessarily espouse Torrey's 'seven easy steps'. Nor do such people always believe that the baptism is authenticated by tongue-speaking. Nor again need they believe in the permanence of the charismata.

It is fair to say, however, that each view reflected here is held by some Christian or other. It is also fair to say that the belief that Spirit baptism is an experience distinct from conversion is the core doctrine of Pentecostalism and that those who hold it seldom stop short of buying the whole Pentecostal package. (Dr Lloyd-Jones, of course, did stop short). Again, it is fair to say that the soil in which this doctrine grew was Perfectionism and that Dr Lloyd-Jones' espousal of it while so vigorously opposing traditional Keswick theology was a historical oddity (made possible, probably, by his taking Spirit baptism out of the realm of sanctification and placing it in the realms of assurance and preaching power). In showing the historical connections of the Doctor's thought we were not suggesting that he was either a Pentecostal or a Perfectionist.

Not Experimental

Others have claimed that the view of Spirit baptism found in these pages is not experimental. This appears to have arisen from a misunderstanding of the argument that the *sealing of the Spirit* in Ephesians 1.13 was objective, not subjective. The point we were making is that the Spirit is not the One who seals but the One we are sealed with. It is Christ who seals, *with* the Spirit. The seal is objective in the same sense as a mark in the forehead is objective. Christ gives us the *real* Spirit, not just a feeling or a mood. When He indwells us He does not lose His own personality in ours. He retains His own distinctness as surely as the Christ who indwells our hearts by faith (Eph.3.17). On the other hand, to be sealed (or filled or baptised) is undoubtedly an experience. It is something that happens to us and in us and which leads to other experiences, such as peace with God, assurance of His love and participation in His power.

Whether Spirit baptism besides being *experiential* is also vivid and unforgettable is another question. It is true that virtually all the experiences of Spirit baptism recounted in the new Testament were distinctly memorable: Pentecost, Cornelius, the Ephesians. But then, we must remember that no distinction can be drawn between being baptised and being filled; or between either of these and receiving the Spirit or having the Spirit come upon us. Are we then going to say that receiving the Spirit is always a conscious and memorable experience?

Furthermore, if it is fair to infer from the Book of Acts that Spirit baptism is always a conscious experience it is equally fair to infer that conversion is always a conscious and memorable experience. There are of course many who take this position and it is highly plausible. Where in the New Testament is there an instance of an unconscious conversion: the Ethiopian? Saul? Lydia? the Philippian jailer? But the argument is not really as strong as it looks. In the very nature of the case the New Testament records only what was open and well known. Quiet, gradual conversions (assuming there were any) were neither newsworthy enough nor conspicuous enough to be recorded. Such a testimony as Cesar Malan's, for example ('God awoke me as a mother wakens a child: with a kiss') may be beautiful, but it is unobservable and unreportable. All we are left with, therefore, is an argument from silence. There is no recorded instance of an unconscious experience of baptism in the Holy Spirit. But what if in the nature of the case there could be only silence? Suppose there were thousands of gentle, gradual awakenings (or Spirit baptisms). Could they have been recorded?

Second Generation

There is another difficulty, too. The Book of Acts tells us little or nothing of the experience of second-generation Christians. This is a matter to be treated with caution. It would be utterly wrong to set Acts over against the didactic parts of the New Testament (notably the epistles). Acts is part of the canon and we accept its theological authority unreservedly. Time, however, does make a difference. There are *first* Christians. There is an apostolic age, different from all succeeding ages. There is a Day of Pentecost, different from all the days after Pentecost. There is a day when the gospel first breaks through to the Samaritans; another when it breaks through to the Gentiles; yet another when it breaks through to Europe. It is in this great series of *firsts* that Acts is interested and the experiences associated with them were inevitably dramatic. But what of the second generation? What of the children? Were their experiences equally dramatic? And are those brought up in Christian homes today to have experiences as memorable as those of Cornelius and Lydia?

All pastors know that there are many members in their churches for whom conversion (and, on our understanding, Spirit baptism) was not a memorable conscious experience. Are we simply to deny the Christian standing of such people? Or can we find anything in the New Testament to help us understand their position?

First, there is the experience of John the Baptist, who was filled with the Spirit from his mother's womb. It was certainly not for him a conscious or memorable experience.

Second, there are many of whose conversion we have no account. Among these the case of Timothy is especially interesting. From his earliest years, he had been familiar with the Scriptures, 'which are able to make thee wise unto salvation' (2 Tim. 3.15). Is this what actually happened: nothing dramatic, but a gradual yielding to the force of truth expressed in the Scriptures themselves?

Third, there is the New Testament attitude to the basis of assurance. There is no doubt that, other things being equal, the soul is conscious of its own faith. Nor is there any doubt as to the vital role of the Holy Spirit in witnessing to our sonship. Neither, however, is there any doubt as to the necessity of self-examination: 'Examine yourselves as to whether you are in the faith, test yourselves' (2 Cor. 13.5). Such self examination would hardly be necessary if conversion were always a dramatic or at least memorable experience. Moreover, it is not to something dramatic that the self-examination is to be directed. The questions to be asked are far from spectacular: Do we love the brethren (1 John 3.14)? Do we share in the defence and confirmation of the gospel (Phil. 1.7)? Have we supplemented our faith with virtue, knowledge, temperance, patience, godliness, brotherly kindness (2 Peter 1.5-7)? Do we have the love without which, whatever our knowledge or gifts or experiences, we are nothing (1 Cor. 13.1-3)?

Fourth, there is the language used by the Lord in some of the kingdom parables, especially those in which He compares the kingdom to a seed. The most notable of these is in Mk. 4.26-28: 'So is the kingdom of God as if a man should cast seed into the ground, and should sleep, and rise night and day, and the seed should spring and grow up, he knoweth not how. For the earth bringeth forth fruit of itself; first the blade, then the ear, then the full corn in the ear.' Admittedly, He is speaking of the kingdom in its corporate sense, but when an individual *sees* or *enters* or *receives* the kingdom his experience cannot be much different. For many a Christian, the kingdom comes 'he knows not how'.

Finally, there is the teaching of Scripture on the subject of Christian nurture. In this connection the teaching of the Old Testament is especially important because it is dealing with a settled situation in which children have been nourished in the faith since infancy. The basic biblical attitude is expressed in Proverbs 22.6: 'Train up a child in the way he should go and when he is old he will not forsake it.' We find similar sentiments in Ps. 78.5ff.: 'He established a testimony in Jacob, which he commanded our fathers to make known to their children, so that the generation to come should know them and declare them to their children.' Even in the case of such children, of course, the new birth is absolutely necessary. After all, Nicodemus himself, to whom the Lord spoke so forcefully of the necessity of regeneration, was such a child. But their experience will normally be very different from Abraham's, who had to face the trauma of leaving Ur of the Chaldees, turning his back on his father's house and setting off for an unknown country. The church of the Exodus faced similar trauma. But the experience of their descendants was gentle and undramatic by comparison: too undramatic, as a rule, even to be recorded. It was the same at the beginning of the New Testament dispensation. The apostles and most other Christians of their generation faced drama comparable to Abraham's. But their successors are often led quietly into the kingdom. Their experience is more like Samuel's than Abraham's. Many are, in the highest spiritual sense, Nazarites from the womb. Others cannot remember a time when they did not seek the Lord. Yet others find it impossible to pinpoint the beginning of their interest in spiritual things or to indicate when that interest came to a climax. The important point is not how our faith originated or how it developed but whether it actually led us to Christ. In the last analysis neither vividness nor the lack of it matters: 'He who has the Son has life; he who has not the Son of God has not life' (1 John 5.12).

Wrong Impression

It would be utterly wrong, however, to give the impression that the spiritual experience of Christians today is always, or even usually, undramatic or that spiritual growth is an uninterrupted but imperceptible progress towards maturity. On the contrary, there are both depths and heights. The Lord's own life is an example of this. It was punctuated by a series of spectacular crises: the baptism, the temptation, the transfiguration, Gethsemane, Calvary. On a lower plain the life of the believer follows the same pattern. There are depths (Psalm 130). There are backslidings. There are renewals and restorations. There are answered prayers and great deliverances. There are moments of overwhelming assurance, clear vision and ardent longings. To deny a particular theory of Spirit baptism is not to deny any of these experiences. It is only to deny that any of them is what the Bible means by baptism in the Spirit. It is also to deny that an experience is authentically Christian (or spiritual) simply because it is deep and intense. This was something Jonathan Edwards laboured to point out in his *Treatise concerning Religious*

Affections: 'There may be religious affections which are raised to a very high degree and yet have nothing of true religion.' He could even quote his grandfather, Solomon Stoddard, to the effect that 'common affections are sometimes stronger than saving.'

CHAPTER 1

Baptism in the Spirit

Until the 20th century theologians paid little attention to the phrase *the baptism of the Holy Spirit:* and the relative neglect could claim some biblical justification. The precise wording *the baptism of the Spirit* does not occur anywhere in the New Testament and the idea itself occurs very infrequently. There are in fact only three references: in Matt. 3: 11 (and parallels) where John the Baptist proclaims that Christ will baptise in the Holy Spirit; in Acts 1: 5 where our Lord Himself promises that the disciples will be baptised in the Holy Spirit; and in 1 Cor. 12: 13 where Paul affirms that all Christians were baptised in one Spirit.

The importance of a doctrine cannot be measured, however, by the frequency with which a precise wording occurs in Scripture. Otherwise the doctrine of the Trinity would have to be dismissed as quite secondary. Holy Spirit baptism is only one of several designations for that all-important initiatory experience by which the Holy Spirit comes to take up residence in the believer; and as such it rivals union with Christ as the single most important concept in the Christian doctrine of salvation. Its importance has been further enhanced by the exigencies of controversy and particularly by the construction put upon it by Pentecostal and Neo-Pentecostal theology. This has raised questions so radical and so far reaching that none of us can afford to ignore them.

The most fundamental of these questions is that of the relation of Holy Spirit baptism to regeneration and conversion. Pentecostal theology insists that the two are quite distinct; that the baptism is frequently, if not indeed normally, subsequent to conversion; that it is therefore perfectly possible for a man to have been born again and

yet not have received Holy Spirit baptism; and indeed that
some Christians never receive this blessing.

One of the most articulate advocates of this point of
view was R. A. Torrey, whom F. D. Bruner has described
as 'after Wesley and Finney, the most important figure in
the pre-history of Pentecostalism'. 'The baptism with the
Spirit,' writes Torrey, 'is a work of the Holy Spirit distinct
from and additional to His regenerating work. In other
words, it is one thing to be born again by the Holy Spirit
and quite another thing to be baptised with the Holy
Spirit.' Ralph M. Riggs, a contemporary Pentecostal
theologian, is equally emphatic: 'Although all believers
have the Holy Spirit, yet it still remains that all believers,
in addition to having the Holy Spirit may be filled with or
baptised with the Holy Spirit.' The disciples before Pentecost 'had received the Holy Spirit already, but they yet
needed the baptism in the Holy Spirit.'

Receiving, being filled, being baptised

One major difficulty which immediately faces this doctrine is that the language of the New Testament simply
will not allow us to distinguish in this way between being
baptised in the Spirit and receiving the Spirit. These —
and other terms — are used quite interchangeably. For
example, in Acts 1: 5 Luke foretells the day of Pentecost as
an experience of being *baptised in the Spirit*. In Acts 2: 4 he
describes it as being *filled with the Spirit*. We cannot, in the
face of these statements, go on to say that being filled and
being baptised are two different experiences. On the other
hand, the same experience is foretold in Acts 1: 8 as the
Holy Spirit *coming upon them*; and described in Acts 2: 38
as *receiving the Spirit*. Putting all these together we have to
conclude that having the Spirit come upon us, receiving
the Spirit, being filled with the Spirit and being baptised
in the Spirit are one and the same experience.

The way that Luke describes the experience of Cornelius and his household is equally significant. He sees it as

an exact parallel to Pentecost (Acts 11: 15) and as a precise fulfilment of our Lord's promise. 'Ye shall be baptised in the Holy Spirit' (Acts 11: 16). Yet in describing the event he does not use the language of filling or baptism. He says instead that the Holy Spirit fell on them (Acts 10: 44), that the gift of the Holy Spirit was poured out on them (Acts 10: 45) and, most significantly of all, that they simply received the Holy Spirit (Acts 10: 47).

It is surely clear that no one can claim the authority of the New Testament for distinguishing between receiving the Spirit, on the one hand, and being baptised or filled with the Spirit on the other. Equally clearly, no one can claim canonical authority for the form of words. 'All have received the Spirit, but not all have been baptised or filled with the Spirit'.

All believers baptised in the Spirit

But the case does not rest on biblical vocabulary alone. There is considerable direct evidence in the New Testament that all believers experience Holy Spirit baptism.

To begin with, the universality of the gift of the Spirit was one of the main points in the prophecy of Joel (2: 28-32), of which Pentecost was the fulfilment. In the old dispensation, the Spirit and His gift were distributed only to special individuals within the people of God. This limitation, says Joel, would be done away with in the last days (the Christian dispensation). The Spirit would be poured on all flesh. Their sons and their daughters would prophesy, their young men would see visions and their old men would dream dreams. The Spirit would come not only on the eminent, but on servants and maid-servants. Moses' longing (Num. 11: 29) would be fulfilled: All the Lord's people would be prophets, speaking forth the wonderful works of God.

Luke's account of Pentecost makes it clear that this is exactly what happened: *All* the believers were baptised in the Spirit (Acts 2: 4). The *all* is so defined that it does not allow us to believe that any single disciple was excluded. The whole church described in Acts 1: 13-26 were 'all with one accord in one place', and when the baptism came it came on all of them. At that moment, there was not a single believer in the world who was not baptised in the Spirit. Bearing in mind also his use of Joel's prophecy it is difficult to resist the conclusion that Luke wants to establish at the outset that this is to be the distinctive feature of the new dispensation.

The description of the experience of the 3,000 converted through Peter's preaching is certainly in accord with this. He promised that those who responded to his message would receive the gift of the Holy Spirit (Acts 2: 38). But he does not portray this as something additional to the basic experience of salvation. Instead, the gift is said to be a direct and immediate effect of conversion: 'Repent and be baptised every one of you in the name of Jesus Christ for the remission of sins and ye shall receive the gift of the Holy Spirit'. Remission of sins and the gift of the Spirit go together. A few verses later, the total experience of these converts is said to be simply that they 'gladly received his word' (verse 41). It is fair to conclude from this that the only condition of being baptised in the Spirit is a glad reception of the gospel. Every penitent — every forgiven sinner — has undergone Holy Spirit baptism.

It is the very same doctrine we appear to have in 1 Cor. 12: 13, 'For in one Spirit were we all baptised into one body'. Some have expressed reservations as to the relevance of this passage to the question of baptism in the Spirit and suggested that it refers to baptism *by* the Spirit rather than to baptism *in* the Spirit. It is difficult to see any reason for this. Grammatically, the expression is exactly the same as in Acts 1: 5. Had Paul wished to express the idea of baptism *by* the Spirit he could have done so unambiguously by using the preposition *hupo* (by) rather than the preposition *en* (in). But had he done so, he would have been saying something the New Testament does not say anywhere else. Its uniform teaching is that it is Christ who baptises. In Matt. 3: 11, for example, John the Baptist says, 'He will baptise you in the Holy Spirit'. Peter speaks to the same effect in Acts 2: 33. The exalted Christ has shed forth the Holy Spirit. The only alternative to this is that sometimes (e.g., Acts 1: 4) the Spirit is represented as the gift of the Father. The Spirit Himself does not baptise. He is what we are baptised *in* or baptised *with*. Otherwise it would not be possible to contrast Spirit baptism with baptism *in* (not by) water or to relate it to baptism *in* (not by) fire.

This interpretation is confirmed by the second part of the verse: 'we were all made to drink into one Spirit'. The Greek verb underlying our English is *epotisthemen*. It was frequently used with the meaning of watering (plants) and as T. C. Edwards points out, this metaphor, expressing the ideas of abundance and power, would be perfectly appropriate here: 'Like plants, we are drenched in the Spirit. The one shower waters all the fields and soaks through to the rootlets of every particular blade of grass.' Michael Green combines what he sees as the meaning of the two metaphors of 1 Cor. 12: 13 in the statement: 'All alike have been immersed in the sea of the Spirit; all alike have had His living water irrigating their parched lives.'

The purpose of this baptism Paul defines in the phrase 'into one body'. He uses the preposition idiomatically, in the sense of *'with a view to'*: 'We were all baptised (immersed, drenched, irrigated) in the one Spirit with a view to our forming or becoming one body'.

This surely rules out an elitist interpretation along the lines that Spirit baptism is an experience of the few. All believers are members of the one body and as such all are baptised and all are drenched in the one Spirit. Equally, all have spiritual gifts which are essential to the proper functioning of the body so that no one should feel superior, no one should feel inferior and, above all, no one should feel redundant. It is difficult to see how Paul's argument for recognition of their inter-relatedness and inter-dependence could survive if the body were divided by such a radical distinction as that some had Holy Spirit baptism and some did not. Such a distinction would do exactly what Paul wants to avoid — create a schism in the body (1 Cor. 12: 25).

Theological arguments

The argument that it is possible to be regenerate and yet not possess Holy Spirit baptism is as difficult to sustain on the theological level as it is on the exegetical. All Christians are united to Christ. To suggest that this can be so without a corresponding union with the Holy Spirit is to separate these two persons in a way that is quite inconsistent with historic trinitarian theology. The Son and the Spirit are, with the Father, one God. So close is the union that each is in the other (John 14: 10), so that the mission of the Comforter is equally the mission of the Son (John 14: 18) and Paul can even say, 'The Lord (Jesus Christ) is the Spirit' (2 Cor. 3: 17). It was upon such passages that the post-Nicene Fathers built the doctrine of the *coinherence* of the divine persons. We have a fine statement of the doctrine in Basil: 'If any one truly receive the Son he will find that He brings with Him on the one hand His Father, on the other the Holy Spirit. For neither can He from the Father be severed, who is of and ever in the Father; nor again from His own Spirit disunited. For we must not conceive separation or division in any way; as if either the Son could be supposed without the Father, or the Spirit disunited from the Son.'

If this doctrine of the *coinherence* is true, as it surely is, there can be no relation with the one Person that is not equally and symmetrically a relation with the others. To be fully in the Son is to be fully in the Spirit. To have Christ dwell in our hearts by faith is simultaneously to have His Spirit in our inner man and to be filled with all the fulness of God (Eph. 3: 16-19).

To change the perspective slightly: to be in Christ means to have communion with Him and this in turn means that we share fully in all that He has. The most precious of all His endowments, surely, is the full and overflowing indwelling of the Holy Spirit. The Pentecostal argument wishes us to believe that we can be in Christ and yet not share in this; or at least, not share in it fully. But this, surely, is impossible. How can He be said to share if He withholds His Spirit, or bestows Him only 'by measure' (John 3: 34)? To be a member of His body means, if the metaphor has any significance, that we share fully in His vitality. It is His spiritual life that courses through us, enabling us to say, 'Christ lives in me' (Gal. 2: 20). We are rooted in Him (Col. 2: 7), our roots going deep into the resources of Christ so that we effectually tap the fulness of the Spirit that is in Him.

The New Testament view of faith

The Pentecostal position is equally inconsistent with the New Testament view of faith. Faith saves; and it is impossible to confine this to regeneration and conversion, excluding the gift of the Spirit. The Spirit is the unspeakable gift (2 Cor. 9: 15). He is the paramount promise of the Father (Acts 1: 4) and the invariable seal upon our sonship (Eph. 1: 13). Sharing Christ's experience of Him is the climax of the apostolic benediction (2 Cor. 13: 14). Even to the Old Testament, salvation could not be defined apart from receiving the Spirit: 'I will put my Spirit within you, and cause you to walk in my statutes' (Ez. 36: 27).

But not only does the New Testament insist that baptism in the Spirit is part of the very meaning of salvation. It also asserts explicitly that faith and the gift of the Spirit are inseparably connected. This appears clearly in Paul's rhetorical question in Gal. 3: 2: 'Received ye the Spirit by the works of the law or by the hearing of faith?' He lays down the same doctrine in Eph. 1: 13: 'In whom also, after ye believed, ye were sealed with the Holy Spirit of promise'. All they did was to believe: having done so, they were sealed. Gal. 3: 14 is clearer still. We receive the promise of the Spirit through faith. Part of the interest of this passage is that it equates the *promise of the Spirit* with the *blessing of Abraham*. In other words, the gift of the Spirit was the core of the blessing promised in the Abrahamic covenant. We cannot be beneficiaries under that covenant and lack it. Nor can we conceivably be children of Abraham and lack it. Indeed, we can go further still and argue that the conferring of the Spirit was the great purpose of the atonement and that we can have no share in the blessings of that atonement without having the fulness of the Spirit. The movement of Paul's thought is quite clear: 'Christ has redeemed us from the curse of the law . . . that we might receive the promise of the Spirit through faith.' We cannot let ourselves be put in the position where, before qualifying for the gift of the Spirit, we must have something additional to faith — some *plus*. Faith puts us in Christ and by doing so makes us nothing short of complete (Col. 2: 10).

Christian service

It is just as impossible to reconcile the notion that some Christians do not possess the fulness of the Spirit with the New Testament teaching on Christian service. R. A. Torrey tries to make a distinction between being saved and being ready for service and permits himself the following astonishing statement: 'Now if a man is regenerate he is saved. If he should die he would go to heaven. *But though he is saved he is not yet fitted for God's service'* (the italics are his). This distinction does such violence to New Testament theology that one can only gasp. Far from arguing that because not all have the Holy Spirit not all are ready for service we should have to argue that because all are deemed to be ready for service all must be endowed with the Spirit. The Sermon on the Mount, for example, makes clear that Christ expects from every believer the highest standards of service. Every 'blessed' man will live in such a way as to be the salt of the earth and the light of the world (Matt. 5: 13f.). Paul's expectations are similar. He would find the idea of a Christian who is not fitted for service absurd! To be redeemed from sin is to become at once a servant of righteousness (Rom. 6: 18), bearing the fruit of the Spirit in a life characterised by love, joy, peace and all other excellences (Gal. 5: 22f.). Peter is equally explicit: How could the idea of people being saved and yet not ready for service possibly fit into 1 Peter 2: 9: 'Ye are a chosen generation, a royal priesthood, an holy nation, a peculiar people: that ye should show forth the virtues of Him who called you out of darkness into His marvellous light'? The duty of proclaiming the virtues of God is laid firmly on every Christian: but only because of what they are. The imperative rests on the indicative. We are neither exempt from service nor unprepared for it.

The passage from 1 Peter reminds us that among all the various forms of service expected of the Christian, witnessing has a special place. We have to hold fast our profession (Heb. 4: 14), hold forth the word of life (Phil. 2: 16) and give a reason for the hope that is in us (1 Peter 3: 15). This takes us right back to the commission given to the church in Acts 1: 8, 'Ye shall be witnesses to me both in Jerusalem, and in all Judea and in Samaria and unto the uttermost part of the earth.' It was precisely to prepare them for this that the promise was given, 'Ye shall receive power'; and this was the promise fulfilled at Pentecost when the Holy Spirit fell on each of them, enabling them to speak forth the wonderful works of God. Witness — and indeed doxology — is the business of every Christian. To suggest that some believers have been left without the resources for it is to stand the New Testament ethic on its head: as if God expected us to make bricks without straw.

Never an apostolic prescription

Finally, it is surely significant that none of the New

Testament writers, facing the perplexing problems of the early church, ever suggested that what they needed was baptism in the Holy Spirit. Consider the churches they were writing to: Galatia, Corinth, Colossae, Ephesus, Laodicea. Their problems were surely serious enough — disunity, heresy, immorality, worldliness, lack of evangelistic concern. There was an all too evident absence of power. The classic Pentecostal analysis of the luke-warm church at Laodicea, for example, would have been that they lacked 'the fire', 'the second wind', 'the baptism of the Holy Spirit'. But this is never the New Testament approach. Their problems are seen not as due to the lack of Spirit baptism but to a failure to reckon with the implications of the deepest spiritual truth about themselves (Rom. 6: 2, 1 Cor. 6: 2, Gal. 3: 3). It was the very fact that they had all received the Spirit that made their heresy, factiousness and worldliness so appalling.

What then are we to conclude? That baptism in the Spirit is an absolutely fundamental element in the Christian doctrine of salvation; that the experience of it is what initiates a man into the Christian life, so that without it we are not Christians at all; and that to have had it is to have received the Spirit in His fulness, enabling us to say, 'I can do all things in the One who strengthens me' (Phil. 4: 13).

CHAPTER 2

But . . .

There are, however, several passages in the New Testament which appear to support the Pentecostal doctrine of Holy Spirit baptism. We must now examine these.

The baptism of Christ

The boldest appeal is to our Lord's baptism, which Ralph M. Riggs, for example, cites as evidence of a two-tier experience of the Holy Spirit. Jesus was born of the Holy Spirit from the Virgin Mary's womb and for thirty years was the Son of God in a sense that no one else had been. But only at the River Jordan was He baptised in the Spirit; and only then did He receive the anointing from on high which launched Him upon and maintained Him in that most dynamic ministry.

The first point to be made in answer to this is that if it is perilous at all times to take the experience of the non-sinful Christ as typical of the experience of sinful man it is especially so in this instance when we are looking at the relationship between Holy Spirit baptism and the new birth — an experience which the Lord, from the nature of the case, never had.

Second, it is very difficult to believe that the Lord was not filled with the Holy Spirit until His baptism. This would have meant that up to that point He lacked an experience enjoyed by some fairly ordinary believers of the old dispensation, such as Elizabeth (Luke 1: 41) and Zacharias (Luke 1: 67). More important, it would have left the Lord inferior in spiritual experience to John the Baptist, who was filled with the Holy Spirit from His mother's womb. Such inferiority is in the highest degree unlikely, especially when we remember that the Pentecostal argument also involves the claim that the reason why many disciples lack the Spirit's baptism is that they are not 'fully surrendered'.

Third, modern scholarship is inclined to exaggerate the importance of the commencement of the public ministry. Christ's work did not begin with His baptism. For thirty years prior to that, He had been offering to God the sacrifice of His own patient suffering and meticulous obedience, neither of which would have been possible to one who had received the Holy Spirit only 'by measure' (John 3: 34).

But if His baptism did not mark the point at which our Lord was decisively filled with the Spirit, what could its significance have been? The most likely possibility is that it was a fresh enduement with spiritual power granted as preparation for a critical new phase in His life. It is quite clear from the New Testament that those who have been filled with the Spirit can be filled again. Peter, for example, having already been filled at Pentecost is filled again in Acts 4: 8; and in the light of Luke 12: 11, 12 all Christians have the right to expect that at critical moments they will receive special spiritual help. For Christ, the baptism marks the transition to a new phase of His work and, on its threshold, He is given a two-fold comfort: first, that He is the Son of God, assured of His Father's love, help and approbation; and, secondly, that the Spirit is with Him and abides upon Him. The descending dove is the sacramental pledge that Christ is not only burdened with the task of inaugurating the Kingdom but equipped with the powers of the age to come.

Pentecost

A more hopeful argument for the view that baptism in the Spirit is quite distinct from conversion can be derived from the disciples' experience at Pentecost. The account seems to show, as Riggs again points out, that although they had *received* the Holy Spirit already they still needed Spirit *baptism*. In the words of Andrew Murray: 'Just as there was a two-fold operation of the one Spirit in the Old and New Testaments, of which the state of the disciples before and after Pentecost was the striking illustration, so there may be, and in the majority of Christians is, a corresponding difference of experience.'

The disciples did, of course, have a twofold experience of the Spirit. But there is one great reason why they can never be regarded as typical: their discipleship straddled two dispensations and as such was utterly unique. In the early days, they knew only the privileges of the old covenant, living in that era when 'the Holy Spirit was not yet, because Jesus was not yet glorified' (John 7: 39). So long as that dispensation lasted, the Spirit baptism of the new covenant was not within the range of possible experiences. Equally, however, once the new dispensation was inaugurated it was inconceivable that these men could be confined within the limits of the old. In their own lives — in their very hearts — they had to experience the transition from one dispensation to another. Pentecost was the threshold, to be crossed once and once only, into the new era. The *once only* needs to be emphasised. Even the most ardent protagonist of the view that there can be 'a Pentecost' in the life of every Christian has to accept that many of the features of the primal Pentecost never occurred again. For instance, the mighty rushing wind, the cloven, fire-like tongues and the miracle of communication which enabled every one in the crowd to understand the message in their own language — these were never repeated.

To speak of present-day experiences as 'pentecostal' is to overlook the unique grandeur of the event. It was one of the decisive moments in the history of redemption, comparable to the crucifixion, the resurrection and the second advent. Luke's description of it is reminiscent of the appearance of Jehovah on Mount Sinai; and Peter sees it as exactly fulfilling Joel's apocalyptic description of the last days: 'I will show wonders in heaven above and signs in the earth beneath; blood and fire and vapour of smoke:

The sun shall be turned into darkness and the moon into blood' (Acts 2: 20f.). To speak of present-day charismatic experiences in these terms would be absurd. Pentecost was a climactic perforation of human history by the divine, a unique point of transition from the era of preparation to the era of fulfilment. As such it affected the original disciples in an altogether unique way, registering itself in their lives in unrepeatable spiritual and theological displacements.

For the experience of the typical, one-dispensation Christian, we have to look not to the original disciples but to the 3000 converted through Peter's preaching. For them there was neither delay nor distinction between being converted and being baptised in the Spirit. And all the evidence we examined previously suggests that that was to be the norm for the new dispensation. To become a Christian meant passing over at once into the age to come and partaking immediately of the heavenly gift (Heb. 6: 4f.).

The Samaritans

The account of the Samaritan disciples in Acts 8: 12ff. also appears, on the face of things, to support the Pentecostal case. Here were people who were believers and who had been baptised and yet did not receive the baptism of the Holy Spirit until the church at Jerusalem sent down Peter and John who 'laid their hands on them and they received the Holy Spirit'.

The trouble with this argument is that it proves too much. These were not people who had not been *filled* with the Spirit but people who had not yet *received* Him. What came to them through the ministry of John and Peter was not the *second* but the *first* stage of an experience of the Spirit. It is questionable whether they were disciples at all before the apostles' visit. Not only had they not received the Spirit but the way their faith is described is highly unusual. We are not told that they believed *in* or *into* or

upon the Lord Jesus Christ but merely that they believed
Philip. Did this mean anything more than that they gave
intellectual assent to the message Philip preached? In the
case of at least one of them it certainly did not. The faith of
Simon the Sorcerer is described in the same terms as that
of the others. Yet in the sequel Peter has to address him in
the solemn words of verse 21: 'Thou hast neither part nor
lot in this matter: for thy heart is not right in the sight of
God.' He remains 'in the gall of bitterness and in the bonds
of iniquity' (verse 23).

But even if we allow that these men were genuine
disciples (giving its full value to the statement in Acts 18:
14 that 'Samaria had received the word of God'), and even
if we allow that they had a two-stage experience of the
Holy Spirit, we still have to be convinced that their
experience was typical. On the contrary, their position,
like that of the disciples at Pentecost, was unique. For the
first time the gospel was moving beyond the bounds of
Judaism. The transition was not signalised by events of
quite the same magnitude as Pentecost. There was no
rushing mighty wind and there were no tongues of fire.
What there was (assuming there was a delay between the
disciples believing and their receiving the gift of the Spirit)
was a departure from the normal order of salvation.
Moreover, it was a departure of a very precise kind: one
that indicated that the Samaritan church could not exist in
isolation from the church at Jerusalem. Only in the fellowship of the apostles and only as part of the one body of
which the Jerusalem church was the primary cell could the
Samaritans experience normal discipleship. Any suspen-
sion of the connection between faith and Holy Spirit
baptism would be due to the need to make that point
absolutely clear as the church broke out of its Jewish
chrysalis.

The conversion of Saul

Some of the questions raised by the experience of the

Samaritans are raised again by the experience of Saul, to which confident appeal is also made by those who want to separate Holy Spirit baptism from conversion. According to the narrative in Acts 9: 7ff. there was a delay of three days between the apostle's Damascus Road experience and his being filled with the Spirit. The question is: Was he in fact converted on the Damascus Road? Several factors suggest that he was not. He had received a revelation only of the awesomeness of the Lord — one that left him prostrate and overwhelmed. Unlike the Philippian jailer, he received no immediate answer to his question, 'Lord, what wilt thou have me to do?' And his emotional condition was utterly unlike that of his Philippian convert. The jailer, having believed in Christ, was in a state of rejoicing (Acts 16: 34). Saul, 'trembling and astonished', was too upset even to eat or drink, his inner darkness as real as his physical blindness. He could only wait apprehensively until told what to do. The first hint of a gospel — of good news — came only in the words of Ananias, 'Brother Saul, the Lord Jesus has sent me so that you might receive your sight and be filled with the Holy Spirit.' This moment, when his blindness (and his darkness) disappeared forthwith was surely the point of his conversion; and it was also the point at which he received the baptism of the Holy Spirit.

Cornelius

The story of the conversion of Cornelius is not usually appealed to by Pentecostals, although it is as relevant to their case as some of the passages already examined. Cornelius was not in the full sense a proselyte to the Jewish faith: he had not been circumcised (Acts 11: 3). Yet he was more than a typical 'God-fearer' (the outer ring of converts to Judaism). His recognition of the God of Israel was no mere formality. He worshipped Him devoutly and expressed his faith in alms-giving and prayer. That he was in good spiritual standing is surely put beyond doubt by

Peter's clear indication in Acts 10: 35 that he was accepted
with God. 'He must have been a genuine believer and a
justified man,' wrote James Buchanan, 'since without
faith it is impossible to please God.'

The question is not why such a man had to have a special
experience of Holy Spirit baptism but why he had to be
'converted' to Christ. The answer surely is that he was an
Old Testament, pre-Kingdom believer; and when the
King came he had to be confronted with Him and brought
to acknowledge Him. He was in the same state as the
disciples prior to their meeting Christ, 'an Israelite indeed
in whom there was no guile'. Because in their case the
encounter with Christ took place when 'the Holy Spirit
was not yet' their Spirit baptism did not coincide with
their recognition of the Saviour. Cornelius, however, is
first introduced to Christ on this side of Pentecost and the
moment he receives the Word the Holy Spirit falls upon
Him. The event, of course, was epoch-making because it
marked the extension of the kingdom to the Gentiles.
Hence the need to have it witnessed by an apostle (special-
ly dispatched to Caesarea for that purpose) and visibly
attested by tongue-speaking 'as at the beginning'.

The disciples at Ephesus

The last case we need to examine is that of the Ephesian
disciples described in Acts 19: 1-6. At first glance, again,
the Pentecostal argument is very strong. Here are men
who were disciples but had not received the Holy Spirit.
But a slightly closer look quickly shows that things were
not quite what they seemed and that this is in fact what
Paul himself discovered. They were very strange disciples. Not only had they not received the fulness of the
Spirit. They had not received the Spirit at all — they had
not even got to stage one of a two-stage experience. In fact
they had never heard of the Holy Spirit. Stranger still,
they had never heard of Christ and Paul has to tell them
patiently that John (the Baptist), to whom alone they

professed allegiance, had taught that people must believe on the One who came after him, namely Christ Jesus. They had been converted to John, not to Christ, and the only baptism they knew was John's pre-Kingdom 'baptism of repentance for the remission of sins'. Their Christian discipleship dates only from the moment of their Christian baptism at the hands of Paul; and their baptism in the Spirit followed immediately afterwards, when the Apostle laid hands on them.

Nothing in any of these passages requires us to abandon the position we took in the previous chapter: Holy Spirit baptism is a privilege enjoyed by every believer. Indeed, it is itself the divine act of initiation which alone makes a man a Christian.

CHAPTER 3

Holy Spirit Baptism: Seven Easy Steps?

We now turn to a second element in the Pentecostal scheme, mainly, the claim that Holy Spirit baptism is given only to believers who fulfil certain conditions. R. A. Torrey devotes two whole chapters of his book *The Holy Spirit: Who He Is and What He Does* to expounding these conditions and states categorically: 'There is a plain path, consisting of seven very easy steps, which any one here can take today, and it is absolutely certain that any one who takes those seven steps will enter into the blessing.'

Accept Jesus as Saviour

The first step towards receiving the Spirit is, we are told, *accept Jesus as Saviour*. We must be right with God.

The one objection to this is that it is proposed only as a first step. Torrey's definition of it is that 'we rest upon the finished work of Christ on the cross of Calvary, upon His atoning death for us, as the sole ground of our acceptance before God'. This is a fine statement of the nature of saving faith and it is certainly absolutely essential to our receiving Holy Spirit baptism. But according to Torrey and his disciples it is not sufficient. Faith alone does not secure the fulness of the Spirit. This strikes at the very heart of the evangelical emphasis on *sola fide*. It means that a man may be justified from all sin and yet Spirit baptism be withheld; that he may be righteous with the righteousness of Christ and yet be denied the fulness of the Spirit; and even that he may be a son of God and yet go without the seal of that sonship — an heir on whom the earnest of the inheritance is not conferred. This is no mere modification of evangelical theology — an advance consistent with its genius. It is its destruction.

The effect, from another point of view, is an intolerable disjunction of Christ from the Spirit. Faith alone receives Christ. But it does not, we are told, receive the Spirit. Yet, according to Paul, to be in Christ is to be 'complete' (Col. 2: 10). The Lord is the Spirit (2 Cor. 3: 17) and it is precisely because Christ and the Spirit are one that the Saviour can identify the coming of the Comforter with His own coming (John 16: 16ff.). If Christ is present wherever the Spirit is present surely the corollary is also true that the Comforter is present wherever Christ is present?

Renounce all sin

The second step towards the baptism of the Spirit is to *renounce all sin*. We must, says Torrey, 'make a clear-cut choice between the *Holy* Spirit and *unholy* sin'.

The exegetical basis for this is slender. Torrey argues that it is implicit in the word *repent* in Acts 2: 38 and slides gratuitously from defining repentance as 'a change of mind about sin' to defining it as 'renouncing all sin'. The command to repent can no more bear this meaning than it can the Roman Catholic, 'Do penance'.

Furthermore, it is curious in the extreme that the renouncing of all sin could be deemed possible *prior* to baptism in the Spirit. Whatever hope there might be of such a victory once the Spirit in His fulness had come into our lives there could surely be no hope of it before. Indeed, it is difficult to see why Spirit baptism should even be deemed necessary in such a case. If we can dispense with the services of the Holy Spirit in the struggle against sin we can surely dispense with them altogether.

What is emerging here is a full-blown perfectionist theology. 'If there is any measure of rebellion against Him,' writes Ralph M. Riggs, 'that issue will have to be settled with a perfect surrender to Him.' The question is: Is such a state possible to the Christian? Experience — and observation — suggests that it is not; and Scripture confirms it. The post-Pentecost, Spirit-filled, Peter has to be rebuked to his face because he is blameworthy (Gal. 2: 11). Paul laments the presence of a law of sin in his members (Rom. 7: 23). And John, already weary with perfectionists, roundly declares that if we say that we have no sin we are simply deceiving ourselves (1 John 1: 8). How, in the presence of these facts, can we say to struggling believers that if only they will take the simple (*sic*) step of eliminating every vestige of rebellion from their lives, surrendering fully to God and renouncing all sin they will then receive the blessing of Spirit baptism? That may comfort the deluded. But it will drive the realist to despair.

Open confession before the world
The next step laid down by Torrey is open confession before the world of our renunciation of sin and of our acceptance of Christ. This invites three comments.

First, confession is a perfectly normal and indeed indispensable part of the Christian life. It is neither the evidence of, nor the gateway into, a higher stage of discipleship, but something God expects of every Christian. In its most basic form the evangelistic message lays down that 'if thou shalt confess with thy mouth the Lord Jesus . . . thou shalt be saved' (Rom. 10: 9). If this is so, Torrey's argument will not suit his case. If Spirit baptism is given to all who confess Christ then it is given to all Christians because all are confessors.

Second, Torrey's argument is an inversion of the biblical order. Confession of Christ is not the meritorious cause of Spirit baptism but its result. It was so at Pentecost: they were first filled with the Spirit and then began to proclaim the wonderful works of God (Acts 2: 4, 11). It was so also in the household of Cornelius: as Peter preached, the Spirit fell on his hearers and they began to magnify God (Acts 10: 44, 46). And this was precisely the way Christ said it would be. He did not promise that, if they witnessed, the Holy Spirit would come upon them, but that the

Holy Spirit would come upon them and that they would be witnesses (Acts 1: 8).

Third, in Torrey's statement there is a subtle distortion of the biblical idea of confession. It has become a confession about ourselves: *we* have renounced sin; *we* have accepted Christ. These are claims about our own spiritual state (and at least one of them is false). In the New Testament confession is Christ-centred: He is great (Heb. 4: 14). The testimony is not that we have renounced sin but that Christ saves from it.

Obedience

The perfectionist strain already referred to appears even more clearly in the fourth step: *obedience*. The biblical basis alleged for this is Acts 5: 32, 'The Holy Spirit whom God has given to them that *obey* him'. One's instinctive attitude to this verse is to relate it to 1 John 3: 23, 'This is his commandment, That we should believe on the name of his Son, Jesus Christ, and love one another'. The gift of the Spirit is given to all those who obey God's imperious evangelistic summons. Riggs and Torrey see it quite differently. To the former, it means perfect surrender. Torrey is even more stringent: 'Obedience is not merely doing one, two or three things that God commands, but doing everything that He commands. . . . This is one of the most fundamental things in receiving the baptism with the Holy Spirit, the unconditional surrender of the will to God'.

We must ask again: Why should such a person need the baptism with the Holy Spirit? Has he not already, by his own strength, done everything for which the Spirit's help might be desired?

But then, anyone who has reached this spiritual level is living on a plane which Scripture never contemplates as possible for the Christian. Only a seared conscience or a benighted theology could persuade any man that he had made an absolute surrender of his will to God and was obeying all His commands. Conversely, the Pentecostal scheme is as if the way to Holy Spirit baptism were guarded, even from the Christian, by the flaming sword that turns every way (Gen. 3: 24). If the condition of receiving the Holy Spirit in His fulness is perfect obedience then God is mocking us: Whosoever shall keep the whole law and yet offend in one point, he is guilty of all (James 2: 10).

Thirst

The fifth condition is *thirst* and for this, too, a text is offered: 'If any man thirst, let him come unto me and drink. He that believeth on me, out of his belly shall flow rivers of living water. But this spake he of the Spirit, which they that believe on him were to receive' (John 7: 37ff.).

In Torrey's use of this passage there is a clear desire to relate Spirit baptism to something meritorious on the human side. In the text itself, thirst is clearly equivalent to faith and it is stated, quite categorically, that Spirit baptism will be given to those who believe. Like justification, the only qualification is faith alone. But this will not suffice for the perfectionist, conditionalist theology of Pentecostalism. It is engaged in a search for something *we must do* to receive baptism in the Spirit; and if all it can find is *thirst* then the thirst itself must be defined in strenuous terms, so that one can look at it with satisfaction. It secures Spirit baptism not as simple thirst but as special thirst; as thirst *plus*. It must be sustained, sincere and intense. Whether, even as such, it is meritorious, is another question. But the attempt to make it is valiant enough: 'When a man really thirsts,' writes Torrey, 'it seems as if every pore in his body had just one cry, "Water, water, water." When a man thirsts spiritually, his whole being has just one cry, "The Holy Spirit, the Holy Spirit, the Holy Spirit, O God, give me the Holy Spirit".' Furthermore, the desire must be a pure one: 'You must desire the baptism with the Holy

Spirit for the glory of God and not for your own glory. You must desire the baptism with the Holy Spirit in order that you may honour God with more effective service and not merely that you may get a new power or a new influence or it may be a larger salary.'

The whole effect is to shift the emphasis from God's promise and from Christ's work as Surety to some meritorious human quality. We are reminded of the story of Naaman, expecting something spectacular as the condition of having his leprosy cured and given instead the devastatingly simple instruction, 'Go and wash in Jordan seven times' (2 Kings 5: 10). Naaman 'was wroth'; and many Christians seem to find it equally offensive that so glorious a promise as baptism in the Spirit requires for its fulfilment only faith in Christ.

Just ask Him

The sixth condition is 'just ask Him'; or, more specifically, definite prayer for this definite blessing. The prooftext offered here is Luke 11: 13, 'If ye then, being evil, know how to give good gifts unto your children: how much more shall your heavenly Father give the Holy Spirit to them that ask Him?'

It is difficult to see how this can lend any support to the Pentecostal case. It does not refer to baptism in the Spirit but to the mere giving of the Spirit so that, so far as the language is concerned, it amounts to no more than the experience which Torrey describes contemptuously as 'having the Holy Spirit dwelling in us way back in some hidden corner of our being where we are not distinctly conscious of His presence'. It is Torrey himself who distinguishes between the giving and the baptism and on his own terms Luke 11: 13 is quite irrelevant to his argument.

What is happening is that once again the idea of merit — of complying with certain prescribed conditions — is thrown into prominence. Baptism in the Spirit is for those who are worthy, and Riggs does not even have the caution to avoid the use of the term. Referring to James 4: 2 ('Ye have not because ye *ask* not') he writes: 'This is God's elimination test to determine whom He considers *worthy* to receive this priceless gift. It is without money and without price, but He will give it only to those who ask for it.'

Torrey begins with 'Just ask', which, so far as we can see, is no different from faith alone. But his exposition shows that in his view no ordinary asking will suffice. The prayer must be very special, so that once again the focus moves from the divine promises and the divine Surety to the quality of our own asking. Looking back on a typical example of what he has in mind, Torrey writes, 'About midnight God gave us complete victory. And oh! what praying there was from that time on up to a little after two in the morning. I think I had never heard such praying before and have seldom heard such praying since.' That the Spirit is promised to prayer is one thing. That He is promised to *such prayer as one has never heard before* is quite another.

The whole thrust of the Lucan passage is against Torrey's argument. For one thing, the child's need for bread cannot be met by any once-for-all experience. It is a recurring thing, and so, by analogy, is our need of the Holy Spirit, for Whom we have to pray constantly. Again, the child's need is not for some luxury or extra, but for bread — for the staff of life. By analogy, again, the Holy Spirit is Someone whom every believer needs indispensably and Whom God can no more withhold from His children than a human father can withhold bread from his family. Yet again, it is inconceivable that an earthly father would give food to his children only if they asked for it in a special way; or subjected them to some 'elimination test' to make sure they really wanted it — wanted it urgently, fervently, importunately and purely.

The Holy Spirit's ministry, in all its fulness, is, for the

Christian, a matter of survival; and while he is certainly to ask for it he expects to receive it not because of the special quality of his asking but because of the urgency of his need and the certainty of his Father's promise.

Faith

The last step towards receiving Holy Spirit baptism is faith. We may read this with astonishment. How can faith be *last*? But our astonishment would be misplaced. The definition of faith at this point is peculiar. It no longer means trusting Christ crucified, but expecting God to give you whatever you ask. This, according to Torrey, is where many fail, including 'a countless multitude of earnest seekers for the baptism with the Holy Spirit. They meet the other conditions, they pray definitely and earnestly, but they do not confidently expect and therefore they do not get.'

But this either means too little or it means too much. If Torrey is saying that every believer, simply because he is a believer, has a right to expect baptism in the Holy Spirit, he is giving away his own case. On the other hand, to say that absolutely any one who expects Spirit baptism will receive it is saying too much. For example, there are many people who confidently expect to go to heaven who will be sorely disappointed (Matt. 7: 21ff.). We have to ask: Who has the right to expect the blessing? On what is such confidence based? To say, On the confidence itself, is no answer. The only reasonable ground for confidence, in any of our prayers, is the fact that God has made a certain, definite promise to someone in our circumstances. So far as Holy Spirit baptism is concerned, the ground of confidence is that God has promised the fulness of His Spirit to all believers; and only to believers.

Conclusion

Recently, some preachers within the Reformed community have begun to suggest that Calvinists and Char-

ismatics should draw closer together and even unite organically, forming local churches incorporating both traditions. Such proposals can come only from men who regard
charismatic churches as nothing more than typical evangelical churches with tongue-speaking tagged on. The truth
is far different. Long before we get to discussing tongue-
speaking, the theology of these churches differs radically
from that of the Reformation.

First, it is perfectionist: consciously and deliberately so.
'The Pentecostal child,' writes the well-known Anglican
charismatic, Michael Harper, 'was brought up in the
nursery of the Holiness Movement, from which it ac-
quired so much of its teaching — and also, strangely
enough, a great deal of its persecution. Methodism, and its
various ancestors in the Moravian sects, had always taught
both the decisiveness of the conversion experience and
also of a further experience, variously called "entire satisfaction", "holiness", "perfect love", "the second blessing" and later "the baptism in the Spirit". It was largely
from this rock that the Pentecostal stone was hewn.' This
pedigree explains why Pentecostalism believes in the pos-
siblity of renouncing all sin, obeying all God's commands
and surrendering our wills absolutely to His. How can any
one hope to reconcile such an outlook with the sin-
conscious Augustianism of the Reformers and the Puritans?

Second, Pentecostal theology is conditionalist. If we
wish to enjoy all the blessings of the covenant, faith alone
is not enough. One must, in addition, renounce all sin,
obey all God's commands, *really* thirst for the Spirit, *really*
ask and *really* expect. The departure from *sola fide* is
radical and the road to spiritual fulness beset with problems so intimidating that they can be overcome only in the
imagination.

One final comment: How skilfully does the Pentecostal/
Holiness preacher hedge his bets! The promise is glorious.
The steps to it are easy. But if the hearer does not secure it

there can be no come-back on the preacher. He can always say: Ah! But you have not renounced *all* sin. You are not *fully* surrendered. You do not *really* thirst. You do not ask *purely*. You do not *confidently* expect. The resulting agony to the spiritually desperate is no different in principle from Luther's self-flagellations.

CHAPTER 4

Have Spiritual Gifts Ceased?

So far we have said nothing about the most controversial of all Pentecostal claims, namely, that the proof of Holy Spirit baptism is the possession of certain *charismata* (spiritual gifts), especially the gift of tongues. Protestant-ism had traditionally taken the view that miraculous gifts ceased with the apostolic age. Edward Irving (1792-1834) asserted, however, that the gifts were for all ages of the church and through his influence a group of Christians in London set up the Catholic Apostolic Church, complete with apostles, prophets, healings and tongue-speaking. Irving's movement petered out, but in the 20th century, out of the Wesleyan-derived holiness movement, there arose the Pentecostal churches, holding, according to one of their leading spokesmen, that, 'Speaking with tongues is the only evidence in the Scripture of the baptism in the Spirit.' Since the Second World War adherents of this view have multiplied within the mainstream denomina-tions, giving rise to so-called Neo-Pentecostalism. Re-formed churches have not been exempt and many inde-pendent fellowships in England and Wales have been tragically split over the issue.

Any biblical response to this movement must insist on two fundamental points: First, some of the charismata have ceased; second, the church today remains a thor-oughly charismatic institution. This chapter can deal only with the first of these but we must bear in mind that in the long term concern with the positively charismatic nature of the church is infinitely more important than the denial of modern charismatic claims.

The apostolate

The Pentecostal position requires the perpetuation of the exact situation which prevailed in the apostolic church. In particular, it requires that we must have all the gifts, all the experiences and all the offices enjoyed by the primitive community. The hopelessness of this claim becomes apparent, however, the moment we reflect on the office of apostle. Their *charisma* was clearly intended to be temporary, if only because it was an essential qualification that they should have seen the risen Christ. This is why Peter lays down in Acts 1: 21-22 that the person chosen to replace Judas must be 'a witness with us of his resurrection'. Paul clearly related his apostleship to the same fact: 'Last of all, he was seen of me also, as of one born out of due time. For I am the least of the apostles' (1 Cor. 15: 8, 9). The Galatian denial of his apostleship also revolved around this issue: He was no real apostle because he had never seen Christ and had received his gospel only at second-hand. Paul protests vigorously that he had not received his gospel from men but had been taught it by a revelation of Jesus Christ (Gal. 1: 12). His call to be an apostle was intimately bound up with his having seen the Son of God (Gal. 1: 16).

The argument from the unrepeatable nature of apostolic qualifications is reinforced by the fact that the apostles never designated successors; nor did they lay down the qualifications such successors should have. They were content to leave the founding of new churches to evangelists and the care of existing ones to pastors and teachers. The nearest we have to a successor to the apostles is Timothy and he is spoken of only as an evangelist, whose authority does not go beyond enacting in the churches the arrangements which Paul lays down.

The temporary nature of the apostolate is implied in its very nature. It was foundational: the church is built 'on the foundation of the apostles and prophets' (Eph. 2: 20). The same idea occurs in Rev. 21: 14, which tells us that the

walls of New Jerusalem had twelve foundations inscribed
with the names of the twelve apostles. It is true, of course,
that the building of the spiritual temple goes on throughout the Christian era (1 Peter 2: 5) as each stone is chosen
and prepared. But the laying of the foundation takes place
once and for all in the period of the incarnation. Christ is
the chief cornerstone. The apostles are the foundation.
The once-for-allness of this is clearly seen in the New
Testament itself. Just as Christ was once offered, so the
faith was once delivered to the saints (Jude 3). Consequently, the proper attitude to apostolic tradition is not to
develop and add to it but to 'hold it fast' (2 Thess. 2: 15). It
is a sacred trust to be kept (1 Tim. 6: 20).

The uniqueness of the apostolic period at the time of
authoritative foundation-laying is integral to the New
Testament and Oscar Cullmann is fully justified in assert-
ing that, 'the scandal of Christianity is to believe that these
few years, which for secular history have no more and no
less significance than other periods, are the centre and the
norm of the totality of time'.

Prophecy

We can claim with virtually equal confidence that the
gift of prophecy has ceased. Prophecy in the New Testament was not a merely expository gift enabling a man to
unfold the meaning of an extant revelation such as the Old
Testament. The prophets were organs of revelation, men
to whom God made known His mind and whom He had
authorised to act as His spokesmen. In the church at
Corinth, for example, they were the men who had a
revelation and 'understood all mysteries'. Sometimes, the
revelation was a prediction, sometimes it was a directive
and sometimes (as in the Apocalypse of John) it was a
sustained and complex disclosure of the mind of God
ranging over a wide variety of topics, doctrinal, hortatory
and eschatological.

We have a right, then, to expect from prophets 'mysteries and revelations'. When we apply this criterion to modern utterances, it is only too painfully obvious that the gift has ceased. The reasons are not far to seek.

First, like the apostolate, prophecy was foundational. The foundation referred to in Eph. 2: 20 is that of the apostles *and prophets*. During the age of foundation-laying the prophets (like their Old Testament predecessors) were producing material which would later be incorporated into the Scriptures. They were also meeting the urgent need for instruction and guidance on a day-to-day basis until the church had a sufficient Scripture. But these responsibilities could not last longer than the age of foundation-laying itself.

Second, even within the New Testament itself there is evidence that the re-instatement of the prophetic office (after the long silence from Malachi to John the Baptist) was only transitional. While it figures prominently in the picture of church-life given in 1 Cor. 12-14 it is almost entirely absent from Paul's last epistles, the Pastorals (Timothy and Titus). It is also absent from other late New Testament documents such as 1 John. This strongly suggests that the ministry of the prophets was being superseded even before the canon was closed.

Third, the prophetic ministry, being revelational, was closely linked with the development of the canon. So long as the canon was incomplete, the church had to have access to the mind of God in other ways, notably through prophecy. Now that the canon is complete, all that is necessary to salvation is either expressly set down in Scripture or may be deduced from Scripture by good and necessary consequence, as the Westminster Confession reminds us. To say that prophecy is still necessary is to say that Scripture is incomplete and imperfect and therefore needs to be supplemented. Whether the supplementation is offered by Pentecostal prophets or by Papal decrees, the principle is the same: the conscience of the church is being bound by something additional to Scripture.

Tongue-speaking

Tongue-speaking has a special place in Pentecostalism, not only as the commonest of the gifts but as the initial sign of the baptism in the Spirit, the means of deeper devotion and, all too often, as the supreme object of Christian longing. Despite all the arguments marshalled by the Charismatics, however, we see no reason to abandon the traditional view that this gift also ceased with the apostles.

For example, it seems indisputable that as a matter of fact this gift did disappear. This does not mean that no claims to it were made between the first century and the nineteenth. But these claims were sporadic, localised and debateable. Michael Harper cites Justin Martyr in support of the perpetuity of the gifts. Cullmann, with equal confidence, cites him against. More significantly, in the long period between the New Testament and Edward Irving, the gift of tongue-speaking was never claimed by even the most outstanding leaders in the church. This is true of such Fathers as Athanasius and Augustine, Bernard and Chrysostom; of the Reformers, Luther, Zwingli, Calvin and Knox; and of outstanding modern preachers like Whitefield, Chalmers, Spurgeon and Lloyd-Jones.

This fact of the gift being withheld from outstanding men of God is surely the total answer to the claim made by Wesley (and frequently repeated by Pentecostals) that the reason for the decline in this and other gifts was that 'the Christians were turned heathen again and had only a dead form left'. It is absurd to dismiss either Chalmers and Spurgeon or the churches they represented as dead and lifeless shells of Christianity.

Another fact which weighs heavily against the Pentecostal view is that it is now exceedingly difficult to be sure what exactly the gift of tongue-speaking was. He would certainly be a bold man who would undertake to prove by exegesis of the New Testament that what passes for tongue-speaking today corresponds to the gift which prevailed in the days of the apostles.

There are two levels, at least, of uncertainty.

First, it is far from clear that the phenomenon described in the second chapter of Acts is the same as that of 1 Cor. 14. The one is defined as 'speaking in *other* tongues'; the other as 'speaking in tongues'. In Acts, the speakers were easily understood by the multitude; at Corinth, they could be understood only by those with a special gift of interpretation. At Corinth, they were a sign of God's judgment on unbelievers; there is not a hint of this in Acts. In view of these difficulties, we cannot lightly assume that the two phenomena were the same.

Second, there is uncertainty as to the nature of tongue-speaking itself; and not only is there a lack of agreement as to what occurred in New Testament tongue-speaking, but there is a lack of agreement as to what takes place in Pentecostal assemblies at the present day. According to some Charismatics, the tongues are foreign languages, recognisable as such and in principle translatable. According to others they are a form of ecstatic speech, in which the Christian expresses concepts and emotions which transcend language — what Donald Gee calls, 'an almost spontaneous expression of otherwise unutterable emotion'. Such utterances would not only be untranslatable but un-interpretable. According to yet others, tongue-speaking is 'a manifestation of the Spirit of God employing human speech organs'. On this view, although the utterance has a language pattern the vocal cords are controlled not by the human intellect (which lies *fallow*, 1 Cor. 14: 14, N.E.B.) but by the Holy Spirit.

For the moment it is not important to settle this question of identification. We need only note that there is no agreement among New Testament scholars or among Pentecostals themselves as to what tongue-speaking was — or is. This is passing strange if it was meant to be, in perpetuity, the initial sign of the Holy Spirit baptism. How can I know if I have spoken in tongues when I do not know what tongue-speaking was?

Diminishing importance

We must add to this problem of identification the fact that we can see tongue-speaking diminishing in importance even within the New Testament itself. Within the Book of Acts, taking us up to the time of Paul's first imprisonment at Rome, the gift is fairly prominent. It is still clearly in evidence when the apostle writes his first epistle to Corinth. But in the Pastoral epistles there is no mention of it, although Paul is concerned to lay down the qualifications for office (which do not include tongue-speaking) and to give detailed instructions as to the conduct of worship and the behaviour of Christians in the public assembly. Furthermore, tongues are not mentioned, even as occasions of disorder, in the Lord's Epistles to the Seven Churches of Asia (Rev. 2-3). Nor are they mentioned in the Epistles of John, although these epistles show considerable interest in the ministry of the Spirit.

These facts strongly suggest that the transitionalism which we saw to apply to the gift of prophecy applies equally to the gift of tongues. By the time the canon is complete, tongue-speaking has been virtually superseded.

This is not an argument which Pentecostals will readily accept. It is tantamount, they say, to taking scissors to the Bible and throwing large chunks of it away.

Part of the answer to this is that the portions excised are not all that large because the references to tongue-speaking are remarkably few. Furthermore, to say that tongue-speaking no longer exists in the church is not to say that biblical references to it have nothing to teach us today. For example, eating food offered to idols is no longer a live issue (so far as we know). But the principles Paul lays down in the course of discussing it are still directly relevant to Christian life and practice. Similarly, despite the cessation of tongue-speaking Paul's teaching in 1 Cor. 14 still has much to say on the nature of worship and the use of our continuing gifts.

More important, every Christian accepts in practice

that some parts of the Bible have been superseded. We no longer offer the sacrifices prescribed in Leviticus or cleanse lepers according to the Old Testament ritual. Not even theonomists would *stone* adulterers and Sabbath-breakers, nor administer circumcision nor celebrate the Passover.

But does that not leave the *New* Testament still intact, so that everything for which we can claim a precedent from the New Testament is still binding? The moment we accept, however, that we can no longer have apostles, we have breached this principle. We have recognised that the New Testament church had something which we are not to have. In actual fact, the range of superseded principles and practices is much wider than we might at first expect. Today's missionaries are not bound by the directive of Luke 10: 4, 'Carry neither purse, nor scrip, nor shoes: and salute no man by the way'. Nor are they under orders to confine their evangelism to the lost sheep of the House of Israel (Mt. 10: 6). Similarly, we are not bound by the ecclesiastical arrangements of Acts 2-5, whereby the apostles did all the teaching and all the administration — and the Christians practised a strict community in goods. Even when we look at the attestation of Holy Spirit baptism, we find only what is an embarrassment to Pentecostalism, because the sign in Acts 2: 2-3 was not tongue-speaking alone, but 'a rushing mighty wind and cloven, fiery tongues'. If the tongue-speaking is normative and perpetual, why not the other signs?

The truth is, we simply cannot freeze revelation at Acts 2: 4 or at 1 Cor. 14: 26, any more than we can freeze it at Luke 10: 4 or Leviticus 17. Revelation is progressive and cumulative, and although God never denies the truth of what He revealed earlier, He does enact that some structures and institutions be superseded. 2 Timothy not only has an equal right with 1 Corinthians to be our norm. Wherever they differ, it has a *greater* right to be the norm because it lies further along the line of a cumulative revelation.

The reason for tongue-speaking gradually disappearing is exactly the same as applies to prophecy. It was a revelatory gift. As Pentecostal theologians themselves admit, tongue-speaking plus interpretation equals prophecy: 'In the Spirit, he speaketh mysteries.' As such, it would meet the needs of the church while the canon was being formed, but would give way to the expository ministry of the teacher once revelation was complete.

Unbiblical framework

Space allows only a brief mention of one other argument: the whole theological framework within which Pentecostalism sets tongue-speaking is unbiblical. The claim is not only that tongue-speaking persists in the church but that it is the indispensable initial sign of a special post-conversion baptism in the Spirit which ushers those who experience it into a 'higher life' of deeper devotion, greater power and new-found joy. This perspective is wholly false. As we have already seen, some of the greatest figures in the post-apostolic church never spoke in tongues and would have to be dismissed as second-rate Christians if the Pentecostal doctrine were true. Besides, there is considerable ambiguity in the doctrine. Is baptism/tongue-speaking something secured by our own holiness? or is it the cause of our holiness? Logically, we should expect the latter: Spirit baptism is the pre-condition of the 'higher life'. In fact, the order is commonly reversed. Torrey's 'seven easy steps' include renouncing all known sin and make holiness the condition of spirit-baptism. Wesley's claim that the church lacks spiritual gifts because it is spiritually dead belongs to the same perspective. If the church could revive itself, the Spirit would return.

Two further points may be made.

It is very difficult to argue that tongue-speaking of the type prevalent today is a sign of special Christian spiritual-

ity when, according to many observers, the same phenomenon can be found among non-Christian religions
such as Islam. The same problem is inherent in the
incidence of tongue-speaking among Roman Catholics.
We would not take it on ourselves to deny that many
Roman Catholics are devout, if mis-guided Christians, but
it is difficult to believe that anyone enjoying an outstanding measure of the Spirit's fulness could have so little
insight into Scripture and so little understanding of the
experience of salvation as to adore the host, worship saints
and images, do homage to the Virgin and distance himself
by an anathema from Luther's doctrine of justification.

Last, there is not the least suggestion in the New
Testament that tongue-speaking is a sign of special spirituality. The church at Corinth came behind in no gift (1
Cor. 1: 7). Yet it was beset by a whole host of problems
ranging from disunity to heresy to immorality. It was
certainly not a 'higher life' church. Moreover, in 1 Cor.
13, Paul makes it very plain that it is possible to speak with
the tongues of men and of angels and yet lack love. Christ
Himself speaks to the same effect in Mt. 7: 22. Men may
be able to claim that they have prophesied, cast out devils
and performed miracles — all in the name of Christ — and
yet be total strangers to fellowship with the Saviour. And
when Paul asks 'Do all speak in tongues?', clearly expecting the answer 'No!' he does not give the least hint that the
omission is a grave one which they should instantly seek to
remedy.

CHAPTER 5

Is the Church Today Charismatic?

One of the saddest features of Christian history has been the way that the great epithets applied to the church have been debased to the point where they have become terms of opprobrium. To many people the word *orthodox* suggests at once something dead, formal and sterile. To many others, the word *catholic* serves only to ignite the fires of bigotry. More recently, the word *charismatic* has suffered a similar fate. Because one group of believers has claimed it as exclusively their own, others have renounced it altogether and even come to equate 'going charismatic' with 'going to the Devil'.

But this debasing of our ecclesiastical currency is surely misguided. Every authentic church must be orthodox, catholic and charismatic. Orthodoxy is no more than profession of the truth. Catholicity means that we belong to the one church; Christ has only one. And to be charismatic means simply that we depend for our survival on the graces of the Holy Spirit.

In the present climate, this last is peculiarly important. It would be utterly tragic to react to Pentecostal excesses by losing sight of the fact that the church is charismatic in its very nature. It cannot exist without being charismatic. The word must be used, of course, in its biblical sense. It does not mean the possession of a magnetic charm or a dominating personality or outstanding natural gifts. Nor does it mean speaking in tongues, engaging in disco-type worship and emphasising spontaneity at the expense of order. To say that the church is charismatic is to say that it possesses spiritual gifts and that it depends on these gifts for its effectiveness. How can a church possibly renounce all claims to such a status? It is made up of spiritual people. It constitutes a spiritual temple. Its members do not comprise the wise, the mighty and the noble but the unlearned, the weak and the ordinary. They can serve one another — and the wider community — only in the power of the Spirit, conferring on them a great variety of spiritual gifts. Some of these — the revelatory gifts — have ceased. But the vast majority of them remain: wisdom, knowledge, teaching, counselling, government, leadership, serving, comforting, exhorting, liberality, administration. These are as vital to the church today as to the believers of the first century.

Charismatic ministry

The charismatic nature of the church is most immediately obvious in connection with its office-bearers. Every ecclesiastical functionary is first and foremost a spiritually gifted man. This is perfectly clear even with regard to the Old Testament church. The prophets, the kings, the judges, the priests — all were charismatic figures. The position in the New Testament is the same. Apostleship was a grace, a *charis* (Rom. 1: 5). The other offices are similarly conceived. They were not related to natural ability or to professional training but to the endowments of the Spirit. The teacher had to be 'apt to teach'. The pastor had to have the gift of government. Even those who served tables had to be full of the Spirit.

Sadly the church did not long retain this vision and alternative views of the Christian ministry soon prevailed. The most widespread of these was the sacerdotal, which saw the minister primarily as a priest with *quasi* magical powers. The responsibilities of such a man centred on the sacraments. In the Communion service he transformed the bread and wine into the whole body, soul and divinity of the Son of God, offered them to God as a propitiatory sacrifice and distributed them to the faithful as their spiritual nourishment. In the service of baptism he administered a rite which automatically and invariably regenerated the recipient. Such a man was not a charismatic. He was a Christian witch-doctor.

Presbyterianism, for the most part, escaped this particular distortion. Instead it faced the danger of an unbiblical professionalism. The view tended to prevail that any respectable man of ordinary intelligence could be turned into a minister by proper university training. Furthermore, a man could survive in the ministry by paying proper attention to the ordinary elements of professionalism: careful attention to consumer expectations, diligence in his homework and punctuality in his appointments. The traditional models of such professionalism were the teacher and the doctor. More recently, especially in America, ministers have seen themselves as managerial executives. The vestry has become a boardroom and the church has been run according to the best business methods. The trappings may be different, but the principle is the same as often prevailed in Scotland — the 'lad o' pairts' graduating *via* a schoolmastership to the pastorate of a respectable congregation.

Both of these concepts — the sacerdotal and the professional — involved a betrayal of the New Testament vision. In the apostolic church, the ministry was not remotely sacerdotal. Indeed, the paucity of references to the sacraments is quite astonishing and their relative unimportance is given formal expression in 1 Cor. 1: 17, 'Christ sent me not to baptise, but to preach the gospel'. Nor was the apostolic ministry remotely professional. Apart from Paul, the outstanding figures of the New Testament had little formal education. They were charismatics.

This implied several different factors.

First, the prerequisite for office was the possession of spiritual gifts. This is self-evident with regard to the revelatory offices. No amount of education, experience or common sense could turn a man into an apostle or a prophet. The same was true, however, in other areas. It was not formal training that made a teacher. Training was not unimportant (2 Tim. 2: 2). But it was more fundamental that a man be 'apt to teach' (*didaktikos*). This implied two other gifts: the gift of knowledge and the gift of communication. These were not matters of mere book-learning (although this was not to be despised: Paul had his parchments). They were — and are — a matter of spiritual insight. The charismatic teacher so sees the truth that he loves it. Furthermore, he sees it in its practical bearings and in its pastoral relevance. His gift is not mere knowledge of the truth but skill in applying it to the needs of the people of God so that they are comforted, admonished and inspired.

The communication skills of the Christian preacher are equally charismatic. They are not identical with those of the professional journalist, politician or advertiser. In fact, in 1 Cor. 2: 4, Paul disowns these. Spiritual communication is marked not by its dazzling professionalism but by caring, honesty and boldness.

The same principle can be extended into other areas of Christian ministry. In the church, leadership is not a matter of natural gifts. It is a matter of spiritual wisdom, vision and courage. Those who possess it may be men of great natural diffidence and timidity. But their weakness is counterbalanced by the fact that they wait on the Lord. In the same way, New Testament pastors faced with the pressures of counselling could claim little knowledge of psychology and psychiatry. Nor had they any clinical training. But they had *charismata*. They had the wisdom that came from above. They had the leading of the Spirit. They had a God-given ability to learn the lessons of experience and to apply biblical principles of conduct. To all such men, knowledge of the basic principles of psychiatry might be a very welcome bonus. But no degree of academic competence can ever compensate for the absence of the pastoral gift itself.

Second, within the framework of a charismatic concept of ministry the possibility of success and effectiveness lies only in the Holy Spirit. This is one of the most humbling things in the whole range of the church's experience. Neither natural ability nor academic training nor personal diligence can guarantee effectiveness. The Gospel must come in *word* (1 Thess. 1: 5). But if it comes in word *only*, it is useless. It must come in the demonstration and power of the Spirit (1 Cor. 2: 4) and be preached with the Holy Spirit sent down from heaven (1 Pet. 1: 2). The message must be from the Spirit. The words must be from the Spirit ('words which the Holy Spirit teaches'). The impact must be from the Spirit ('whose heart the Lord opened'). Without this concurrent action of the Spirit we are help-less, even when preaching to Christians. And, to our chagrin, we can never guarantee, manage or command His concurrence. Even in revival situations, every single inst-ance of blessing is a sovereign gift resulting from the loving discretion of God. This is why all programmes for church growth — the ecclesiastical equivalent of 'manage-ment by objectives' — are virtually blasphemous. Such a practice is tantamount to dictating to God the precise number of miracles of grace we expect Him to perform. So far as real and abiding blessing is concerned, we remain totally dependent on the ebb and flow of divine power.

Third, the obligations and the pit-falls of Christian ministry are those relating to a charismatic situation. We need, like Peter at Pentecost, to be filled with the Holy Spirit. We need to stir up (or fan into flame) the gift of God which is in us. We must avoid grieving or quenching the Spirit. We must even live in holy dread of what is always the ultimate possibility — that God will withdraw His Spirit from Saul and His strength from Samson. Sadly, the fact of such a divine withdrawal may often be obscured from the church and from the individual himself. But whether conscious of it or not he will be left with only the empty shell of office. All the glory, all the power and all

the usefulness have departed. He is a cumberer of the
ground.

Charismatic worship

The charismatic nature of the church is also apparent in
Christian worship. This is already indicated in the Lord's
statement to the woman of Samaria in John 4: 24, 'God is a
Spirit and they that worship him must worship in spirit
and in truth'. Both orthodoxy and liturgical propriety are
highly desirable. But they are not enough. Worship must
be in the Spirit. It is possible only for a spiritual man, and
only in so far as at the very moment of our approach we are
filled with the Spirit of God.

Unfortunately, however, we tend to seek this charismatic quality in the wrong direction. Worship is not charismatic simply because it includes guitars, choruses, clapping and dancing. Nor is it charismatic because it is
spontaneous, exuberant and enjoyable. We cannot afford
to base our worship on the pleasure-principle. That would
only be to exchange one form of hedonism for another.
Charismatic worship should be marked by biblical control. The Spirit will not prompt and stimulate us in a way
that contradicts what He has revealed in Scripture. Equally, charismatic worship will be marked by self-control.
The spirits of the prophets will be subject to the prophets.
Biblical worship is not an ecstatic experience in which men
lose all awareness of themselves, the world and God. It
retains its sense of the holiness of God (Is. 6: 3) as One
august, transcendent and intimidating. Our confidence in
approaching Him derives not from the presumption of
over-familiarity but from His own invitation. We come
with devoutness and humility because we come self-
critically. The lips with which we worship are unclean;
and so are the lips of those who worship with us (Is. 6: 5).

The charismatic quality of Christian worship is most
evident in connection with preaching, which as we have
seen, can never be a merely formal, professional or

academic exercise. It is very doubtful whether preaching thus conceived can be fully rehearsed. Indeed, the practice of reading sermons looks suspiciously like an attempt to take the dependence out of preaching and reduce it to something manageable. In authentic preaching there is always an element of anxiety (*ungst*) — a fear and trembling arising from the dread that the Spirit will not keep us and that we shall be left floundering in our own ineptitude. Charismatic preaching depends on a man's being full of the Spirit. The boldness is the Spirit's. The wisdom is the Spirit's. Above all, the power is the Spirit's. He gives the message cogency, pricking the conscience, causing men to tremble, overriding their prejudices, winning the consent of their intellects and opening their hearts to Christ. In the absence of these factors, our oratory and passion, our logic and profundity, have no more hope of success than a farmer sowing seed on the motorway.

The charismatic quality of worship is also evident in prayer. We must pray in the Spirit (Eph. 6: 18ff.). He must teach us what to pray for (Rom. 8: 26), because we are poor judges of our own needs and even poorer judges of what God has made available to us. He it is also who instructs us how to pray — with groanings — and perseverance, but also with boldness and adventurousness. Nor should we overlook the further fact that where prayer is charismatic — where it is from the Spirit — it will comprehend the whole church. It is not concerned only with its own needs or those of its own immediate circles. Every Lord's Day, charismatic worship will pray for 'all saints' — 'all those throughout the world who profess the true faith'.

The charismatic character of worship is equally clear in connection with our praise. The songs we sing are to be spiritual (Eph. 5: 19). So is the way we sing them. This is not a question merely of enthusiasm. Spiritual singing cannot be equated simplistically with hearty singing. We must sing with the understanding. We cannot sing the *de*

profundis of Ps. 130 with the same verve as we sing such
great anthems as Ps. 100 and Ps. 24. There are songs of joy
and songs of grief, songs for muted accents and songs for
thunderous acclamation. In charismatic worship, the
volume and the tempo will be as varied as the truths we
sing and the moods we express. But the volume and tempo
relate only to externals. The real glory of charismatic
worship lies deeper. We make melody from our hearts — a
melody which results from the Spirit's filling us (Eph. 5:
18) and a melody which is quite independent of our
circumstances. The charismatic worshipper gives thanks
always and in all things (Eph. 5: 20).

Every believer a charismatic

Finally, the everyday life of every believer is charismatic. He has been baptised and filled with the Spirit.
Following on from this, every believer has *charismata* with
which he is expected to serve the body of Christ. All do not
have the same gifts, either as to number or as to eminence.
God distributes to each according to His sovereign will.
But none can regard himself as useless or redundant. Each
member has a meaningful role within the body of Christ.
Without his contribution, the body is impoverished — it
depends on what every part supplies when it is working
properly. The contribution of some members may be a
matter of public acclaim. But the others should not feel
discouraged. The organism needs their help, their liberality, their compassion, their encouragement, their inter-
cession, their private counsel or whatever else it is that
God has conferred on them for the sake of the body.

Conversely, every member needs the *charismata* of all
the others. Not even the most honourable can say to any of
the rest, 'I have no need of you' (1 Cor. 12: 21). We must
all be locked into the body, in living contact with the Head
and sustained by its bloodstream. This is something that
Christian leaders should take special pains to remember.
We are sometimes dreadfully isolated, with the result that

we not only cease to understand the other members but deprive ourselves of the countless little services which they have to offer. We, too, need encouragement, rebuke, company and the down-to-earth word that demolishes humbug and pretentiousness. To pretend to self-sufficiency, emotionally and otherwise, is to risk warping our own personalities and ending up in foul spiritual deformity.

It is also part of our charismatic status that each Christian is splendidly endowed to meet the exigencies of his own existence. These can be demanding enough — the sufferings of the present time, the wiles of the Devil, the perplexities of decision-making and the uncompromising demands of the Christian ethic. To reflect on the difficulties is to risk paralysis. But we do not face these things with our own limited resources. We are united to Christ. We are filled with His Spirit. We are irrigated and re-freshed by the floods of His grace (1 Cor. 12: 13). Our potential is not to be measured in terms of our personal character and heredity, our self-discipline, education and upbringing. We are charismatic figures of unlimited potential. Maybe by disposition and temperament we are weak and inadequate. But as charismatics, waiting upon the Lord, we renew our strength. We mount up, with wings, as eagles. We run and are not weary. We walk and are not faint (Is. 40: 31). We have it in us to be more than conquerors — hyper-conquerors — and may even say with Paul: 'I can do all things in the One who is strengthening me' (Phil. 4: 13). Such a man can endure any pain, bear any burden, climb any mountain, overcome any foe.

But there is something greater still: The Christian's character is charismatic. That character is well defined in Gal. 5: 22ff., where all the virtues and attributes of a Christian are described as 'the fruit of the Spirit'. It is worth noting that *fruit* is in the singular. The *works* (plural) of the flesh are manifold and discordant. The fruit of the Spirit is unitary — a cluster of graces linked together indissolubly. Where any of them exists, all of them exist. The fruit is not love *or* joy *or* peace but love *and* joy *and* peace *and* faithfulness *and* all the others. More important, these qualities are the fruit of the Spirit — not of education or environment or culture or ideology. The Christian cannot be explained from below. The whole secret of his life is that he is *spiritual* — not in some instances, but in all; not occasionally, but habitually. What he is follows organically from the indwelling of the Spirit. It develops out of the implanted seed of God. It is the fruit of our being rooted in Christ.

Among other things, this is of enormous importance for our self-image. We may be mere Christians, relatively unimportant members of the Body. But we are not ordinary. We are in the highest degree extraordinary. We belong to the world to come (Heb. 6: 5). We have already tasted its gifts and experienced its power. Our lives are hidden with Christ in God. They are capable therefore of rising as high as their source, to a level of excellence and nobility otherwise undreamt of.

CHAPTER 6

The Sealing of the Spirit

Unfortunately, we were never in a position to imitate Dr Martyn Lloyd-Jones. A recalcitrant tongue, unmanageable lips and a stubborn accent made it impossible. Yet we owe him an immense personal debt and our early admiration of him was unbounded. We thought his understanding of the major doctrines of Christianity unsurpassed and his skill in proclaiming them incomparable. That is still our opinion and we hold it none the less sincerely now that there is a very important area of the Doctor's theology with which we have the temerity to disagree. We devoured all his earlier publications with delight and they became part of the very fabric of our soul. But some parts of the volume *Preaching and Preachers* filled us with misgiving; *Romans: Chapter 8: 5-17* distressed us; and a recent volume, *God's Ultimate Purpose* (an exposition of the first chapter of Ephesians) has convinced us that it is time to speak out.

The problem is the Doctor's doctrine of the Holy Spirit and especially his view of the Spirit's sealing. He is throwing all the weight of his authority and all his powers of persuasion behind the position that the sealing is something subsequent to conversion and that a man can therefore be a Christian without it.

After you believed?

This doctrine is based, first of all, on Eph. 1: 13, which in the Authorised Version reads, 'In whom also, after that ye believed, ye were sealed with that Holy Spirit of promise.' This strongly suggests that sealing is *after* believing and Dr Lloyd-Jones is at pains to stress that the verb underlying the clause, 'after that ye believed' is in the past tense. In fact, it is in the aorist tense and it is an over-simplification to regard the aorist as a simple past. Greek tenses have to do primarily not with the *time* of the action (past, present or future) but with the *state* of the action (complete, incomplete or indefinite). The aorist is the tense of indefinite action. 'It is simple action without representing it either as completed or incompleted,' wrote our favourite grammarian, A. T. Robertson.

The unwisdom of deducing from the aorist participle in Ephesians 1: 13 that there is a clear interval between believing and being sealed is well illustrated in a very familiar clause from the gospels, 'Jesus answered and said (*apokritheis eipen*).' *Apokritheis* is an aorist participle exactly similar to *pisteusantes* (believing) in Eph. 1: 13. Yet it would be absurd to say that the Lord's *saying* was subsequent to the Lord's answering; and even more absurd to hold that it was possible to have answered without having said. In fact, the relation between believing and being sealed is exactly the same as that between believing and being justified. Faith is logically prior to justification but this does not mean that there is an interval between them or that it is possible to be a believer and yet not be justified. Similarly, faith comes before sealing but this does not necessitate any interval between them.

Nor is Dr Lloyd-Jones' interpretation borne out by the context. This whole section of Ephesians is dominated by the statement in verse three that God has blessed us with *all* spiritual blessings. It is very difficult, so soon after such a statement, to claim that some Christians lack a particular blessing, especially one of such importance that the expositor can say, 'It is one of the most vital of all New Testament doctrines with respect to revival and reawakening in the Christian church.' Can we honestly say that we have been blessed with all spiritual blessings when we have not yet been sealed with the Spirit?

Indeed, is it not the very purpose of what follows verse three to expound the meaning of *all spiritual blessings?*

These include election, adoption and redemption. Are we to break off there and say that the sealing belongs to a different order of thought — that it is not part of the *all spiritual blessings* enjoyed by all believers but something quite distinct experienced only by some and perhaps only by a few?

We should also notice the function of the phrase 'in Christ' throughout this passage. We are chosen in Christ, accepted in Him and redeemed in Him. And we are sealed in Him. All these points stand together and there is not the least hint that it is possible to be in Him and yet not be sealed; nor that in order to be sealed we must have something over and above being in Christ.

The way that Paul goes on to describe the Holy Spirit also makes it difficult to believe that one can be a Christian and yet lack this seal. For example, He is the Holy Spirit 'of promise'. He is not given because certain Christians are superior to others. He is given by unconditional promise to believers merely as believers. Is it conceivable that there are some Christians to whom God has not given the promised Spirit? We should remember the background to this phrase in Acts 1:4 ff., 'Wait for the promise of the Father'. That promise was directly linked to the duty of Christian witness: 'Ye shall receive power after the Holy Spirit has come upon you and you shall be witnesses to me.' Are there some Christians who are not duty-bound to be witnesses? Or are there some bound to be witnesses to whom God has not yet given the promised Spirit?

The Spirit is also described as 'the earnest of our inheritance' and this is even more difficult to fit into Dr Lloyd-Jones view of the sealing. As he himself says — and says so well — the earnest is both a pledge that the inheritance will be given and the first instalment of the inheritance itself. It is difficult to believe that there are some Christians to whom God has given no such pledge and no such first instalment.

Equally, the very idea conveyed by the term *seal* makes

it difficult to believe the doctrine now being offered to us. Basically, the seal is a mark of ownership. It is what attests a man as belonging to God. Only those who are Christians are so attested. But presumably, all who are Christians are attested. How else can they be known to belong to God? Does He have unattested and unauthenticated possessions? Furthermore, Dr Lloyd-Jones does not seem to have faced the question whether the sealing of the Spirit is subjective or objective. Does it mean that the Spirit seals us (for example, by giving us a special degree of assurance)? Or that the Spirit is Himself the seal? Everything points to the latter. The earnest of the Spirit, for example, is the earnest which *is* the Spirit and the baptism of the Spirit is not the baptism which the Spirit gives but the baptism which is the receiving of the Spirit and which Christ gives (Acts 2: 33). Similarly, the seal of the Spirit is not the seal which the Spirit gives but the seal which is the Spirit. A man who enjoys the Spirit's indwelling is thereby attested as Christ's. A man who lacks it is none of His.

The argument from biography

Dr Lloyd-Jones reinforces his argument with numerous quotations from the biographies of such men as Flavel, Wesley, Edwards, D. L. Moody, Christmas Evans and even Charles Finney. What these prove, however, is only that these men had, subsequent to their conversions, overwhelming impressions of the love of God. They do not prove that these experiences were identical with what the new Testament means by the sealing of the Spirit or even that these men themselves regarded their experiences as the sealing of the Spirit.

Take, for example, the well-known experience of Jonathan Edwards when, in his own words, 'I had a view that, for me, was extraordinary, of the glory of the Son of God.' It is very difficult to see how this can serve the purpose of the Doctor's argument. For one thing, it was not a definitive, once-for-all experience: 'I have several other times had views very much of the same nature, and which have had the same effects.' Furthermore, overwhelming though the experience was, it was not an overwhelming sense of *assurance* (which is how Dr Lloyd-Jones describes the sealing). The effect it produced was not a sense of the love of God to Edwards himself but 'an ardency of soul to be emptied and annihilated; to lie in the dust, and to be full of Christ alone.' Even more important, Edwards does not define this experience as the sealing of the Spirit and indeed could not because his views on that subject were diametrically opposed to the one we are now considering. He argued strongly against the idea that the sealing was some kind of immediate revelation or suggestion and held instead that it was the effect of grace on the heart, leaving a divine impress from which our sonship could be inferred. God imprinted His own image upon the soul and that image was His seal. This is exactly what Dr Lloyd-Jones does not believe.

How does this differ from Pentecostalism?

It is not only the detailed conclusions of this volume which are disturbing, however — Its whole orientation fills us with foreboding.

How, for example, does all this differ from Pentecostalism? We find the same doctrine of Holy Spirit baptism and the same appeal to certain passages in the Book of Acts, and although Dr Lloyd-Jones does not teach that Spirit baptism is always attested by tongue-speaking he nowhere criticises modern pretensions to that gift. This is all the more remarkable when one considers his sustained and vigorous condemnation of non-experiential Calvinism or dead orthodoxy. The threat posed by the latter is not nearly as serious as that represented by the charismatic movement, which seems set to swamp English evangelicalism in a wave of mindless hedonism. The need of the hour is to confront the new Finneyism. Instead, the most highly respected figure within Reformed theology speaks in such a way that the new charismatics claim him as one of themselves — and with some plausibility.

On another level, the views now being put forward by the Doctor imply a serious disparagement of the ordinary Christian, who is portrayed as lacking the baptism of the Spirit, the sealing of the Spirit and even the earnest of the Spirit. By any standards these are serious defects and yet, allegedly, they characterise most Christians. It is impossible to harmonise this point of view with the New Testament. On the day of Pentecost every Christian in the world was baptised in the Spirit. According to Colossians 2: 10 every believer is complete in Christ, and according to 2 Peter 1-3 we receive 'all things that pertain to life and godliness' in our primary experience of God's saving power. The position of the mere Christian — united to Christ, having the communion of the Father and indwelt by the Spirit — is glorious, and the attempt to detract from it is misguided. Dr Lloyd-Jones is seeking to create a sense of need and even a feeling of guilt and inadequacy which should not exist. He points the ambition of the Christian in the wrong direction, convincing him that without this special experience he is gravely defective and that the major concern of his life should be to obtain it. Instead, the seal of the Spirit, like the presence of Christ, is the presupposition of our Christian lives. It is not what we seek but what we begin with; and what we seek is, in the comfort, light and wisdom of that Spirit, to serve the body of Christ. It is not difficult to imagine the confusion which arises when Christians spend their lives seeking for what they already have and delaying their service until they get it.

The distinction is even more invidious when applied to preachers. It is becoming common now to speak of those who have had *the baptism* and *the fire* and to contrast these favoured beings with the rest of us. But how is the difference to be defined? Is it that they are sublime orators? or that their preaching has a powerful effect upon

the emotions? or that they are more successful evangelisti-
cally? Of course the preacher must be spiritual, not only
enjoying the ordinary indwelling of the Spirit but also
possessing the special charismata necessary to preaching.
He must have a thorough understanding of his message.
He must be apt to teach. He must be bold. He must have
the wisdom from above. But these don't necessarily make
a man eloquent or moving. Nor do they guarantee evangelistic success. In order to have success the Spirit must
come not only on the witness but also on the world,
convincing it of sin, of righteousness and of judgment. No
experience which is personal to the preacher can guarantee
this divine co-operation. A man may be the most spiritual
person on earth and yet know little blessing on his evangelistic labours. It was so with Isaiah and Jeremiah and even
with our Lord Himself. He had the Spirit without measure and yet at the close of His ministry all His converts
could be gathered into one room. Over against the new
cult of the sealed and the baptised we plead for the
recognition of the plodders who endeavour with poor,
lisping, stammering tongues to fulfil a ministry of recon-
ciliation.

But the most disconcerting thing of all is that in Dr
Lloyd-Jones new emphasis we have a reversion to the
theology of *plus*, which in its various forms has bedevilled
the Christian church. For the Galatians, it was Christ plus
circumcision. For mediaeval Catholicism, it was Christ
plus the sacraments. For Wesley, Christ plus sinless
perfection. For Dispensationalism, Christ plus an earthly
millennium. For Pentecostalism, Christ plus Holy Spirit
baptism. Now from within the very bosom of Reformed
theology there comes the same plea for *more*, not merely
for growth or progress but for a new definitive experience
which will put us in a special category.

We reject the whole concept of *plus*. There is nothing
wrong with our resources nor is there any promise of an
experience out of which effectiveness and revival will

automatically flow. Let the ordinary Christians and the
ordinary preachers work away at reforming the church,
building up the altars of God which have fallen down. Let
them realise that they can never be so filled as not to need
to be filled again — and again and again. Let them realise
that no experience can place within *their* jurisdiction and
management the power which opens hearts. That power
always remains God's, even in the case of the most baptised preacher and the most glorious revival.

In our very ordinariness we are complete in Christ. In
that confidence, let us work out our salvation, individual
and corporate, and the gates of hell will not prevail against
us.

CHAPTER 7

Led by the Spirit

Probably no question is put to ministers more frequently than that of guidance: How can we know God's will, especially at critical points in our own lives? The query reflects not only the stress of decision-making but also the widespread confusion which prevails, mainly because evangelicalism has for long been bedevilled by a whole mythology of guidance. Young Christians hear constant references to such experiences as 'being led', 'feeling called', 'the Lord laying a burden' and 'Scripture speaking'. Some believers seem to be told very directly whom to marry, others are given explicit instructions to go as missionaries to precisely designated areas and yet others are called to the ministry by unchallengeable voices from heaven.

Young Christians react to this ideology in two ways. Many quickly conclude that because they lack such experiences they are very poor Christians, if indeed they are Christians at all. Others, more impressionable, seek the experiences they hear so much of, adopt the canonical terminology and soon begin, like everyone else, to feel led and spoken to.

Staggering claims

We are now so familiar with this thought-world as to be completely unconscious of the staggering claims it involves. In effect, the people concerned are saying that they receive special revelations. God has revealed to them that they should marry or change jobs or become ministers or missionaries.

One problem with this is that it puts pressure on the rest

of the Christian community. Revelation cannot bind only
the person who receives it. It binds everyone else as well.
If God has revealed to someone that He is calling him to be
a minister, He is also revealing that He requires the church
to recognise, train, license and ordain him. It then becomes sacrilegious to ask questions implying a doubt or a
desire to test the call. Who are we to question God's
revelation? This probably explains why in every branch of
the church people are admitted to the ministry who are
totally unsuited to the work. How can a mere committee
ask mundane questions about health, academic background, spiritual gifts and working experience of an appli-
cant to whom God has spoken directly?

In fact the claims go beyond what the church enjoyed
even when God was clearly giving her canonical special
revelation. During that time certain men undoubtedly
received direct disclosures of the divine mind. But the
privilege was not common to all believers. It was confined
to prophets who received an audience with God, heard His
secrets and were commissioned to act as His spokesmen.
The rest of the believing community were not spoken to
directly. They received their guidance from the prophets.

Conceivably things might have changed under the New
Testament and every single believer receive special revelation as he receives Spirit baptism. But this is not what we
find. The early church, however enriched beyond the
level of the Old Testament, still had special ministers of
the word. It was guided by prophets and apostles. It was
through prophets, for example, that Paul and Barnabas
were called to missionary work in Galatia (Acts 13: 2). It
was an apostle who was forbidden to speak the word in
Asia (Acts 16:6) and it was an apostle who received the
Macedonian cry (Acts 16: 9). It is perilous to take these
experiences of a few individuals, called to a unique ministry, as models for ourselves. Prophets and apostles existed
precisely because not all members of the church received
special revelation.

It is difficult to see how current ideas on guidance can be reconciled with the position laid down in the Westminster Confession (Chapter One, Section One) to the effect that 'these former ways of God's revealing his will unto his people have now ceased'. We have already seen that these 'former ways' did not mean giving special revelation to every believer. It was confined to apostles and prophets. The point being made here is that this, too, has ceased. God no longer reveals Himself in this way even to prophets and apostles. The language of the Confession is very careful, however. It does not say that revelation has ceased, but only that the *former ways* of God's revealing Himself have ceased. We still have revelation and we still have the ministry of apostles and prophets: but we have them only in Scripture. The Bible is not the mere record of revelation. It is revelation itself, God's word for today. Furthermore, the 'former ways' — the ways which lie behind Scripture — did not cease until 'the whole counsel of God concerning all things necessary for his own glory, man's salvation, faith and life' had been set down in Scripture (Westminster Confession, Chapter One, Section Six). In other words, the reason why God no longer reveals Himself as he did to the apostles and prophets is that in the Bible we have everything we need to know. Hence, says the Confession, nothing is to be added to the Scriptures, 'whether by new revelations of the Spirit or traditions of men'.

The Mind of Christ

But if we rule out guidance by special revelation, what can we turn to? For the moment, we must confine ourselves to two reference-points.

The first of these is the description of the incarnation given by Paul in Philippians 2: 5-11. Behind the enfleshment of Christ lay a pre-temporal decision to become incarnate, and the relevance of this passage to our present enquiry is that it allows us a glimpse into what led the Lord to take that decision. One factor stands out dramatically: His altruism. He did not look to His own things (interests) but to those of others. The same thought lies behind the puzzling words of verse six, as rendered in the Authorised Version: 'He thought if not robbery to be equal with God.' The word translated *robbery* occurs only here in the New Testament and this makes it difficult to define its meaning exactly. Leaving the complicated grammatical and linguistic arguments aside, the problem resolves itself into this: Was being equal with God something the Lord did not have and might be tempted to grasp at (hence *robbery*)? or was it something He did have but was willing to forego?

There can be no doubt on theological grounds that the latter is the correct interpretation. The Lord was equal with God, possessing all the titles, attributes and prerogatives of His Father. But he did not regard this equality as something to be clung to. This was highly relevant to the church at Phillipi, which was being torn apart by disputes relating to status. Everybody knew who and what he was, stood on his dignity and claimed the respect due to his position and years. Christ's attitude was completely different. He had the most exalted status conceivable, but He did not cling to it. He was willing to be sent out from God (Gal. 4: 4) and to make Himself poor (2 Cor. 8: 9).

> That glorious form, that light insufferable,
> And that far-beaming blaze of majesty
> He laid aside; and, here with us to be,
> Forsook the courts of everlasting day,
> And chose with us a darksome house of mortal clay.

The final outworking of this appears in verse seven. The clause translated *He made himself of no reputation* means literally *He emptied himself*. Whenever it appears elsewhere in the Greek Scriptures the verb requires to be translated metaphorically. Here in Phil. 2: 7 the best translation is *He made Himself nothing*. The self-emptying of Christ did not consist in His laying aside something. Instead, the truth is expressed in the startling paradox, *He emptied Himself . . . taking*. It was a subtraction by addition: and what He did take is defined as *the form of a servant, the likeness of men* and *the cursed death of the cross*. He accepted a dramatic reduction in status, undergoing a demotion and degradation so complete that at last His identity was totally obscured and all that could be seen was a man disgraced, disfigured and damned, His death-throes intensified by His terrible sense of alienation from God.

This willingness on the Lord's part to be nothing is decisive for our own theology of guidance. As Christians, we never have the right to put our own interests first. We have to view our options from the stand-point of others, even though this may lead to serious loss for ourselves. God's will, for us as for Christ, may involve a downward rather than an upward movement, demotion rather than promotion. We have no choice. Entry to the Christian life is through the 'strait gate', always too narrow to allow us to bring the baggage of our own egotism through. To be converted is to have accepted in principle the role of a servant, so that our own personal wants and desires can never again be paramount. We live to do God's will and that often meets us as something we shrink from, as the Lord shrank from His cup and Moses, Jeremiah and Paul shrank from preaching.

We may go further. Not only will service come between us and our desires. It may also come between us and our needs, simply because our concern to meet the needs of others makes it impossible to attend to our own. God's will may, for example, cut right across our temperaments. The gregarious may be called to loneliness, the shy to intense publicity, the physically weak to great tests of endurance.

The inescapable fact is that God's guidance always leads to *kenosis:* to that self-emptiedness where one asks only, What will best meet the needs of others?

Christian prudence

The second reference-point in plotting our doctrine of guidance is a neglected but highly important statement in the Westminster Confession (Chapter One, Section Six): 'There are some circumstances concerning the worship of God and government of the church, common to human actions and societies, which are to be ordered by the light of nature and Christian prudence, according to the general rules of the word, which are always to be observed.'

What the divines have in view, of course, is that Scripture, despite its sufficiency as a rule of faith, cannot determine such things as the time and place of public meetings, the order of services, the versions to be read, and the number of office-bearers to be appointed. In these matters we are left to 'the light of nature and Christian prudence'.

But the teaching here is relevant to a much wider area of the Christian life. In fact, it gives us, in brief compass, a very comprehensive theology of guidance.

This involves three principles.

First, we are always to observe the general rules of the Word. We can never appeal to the light of nature or to Christian prudence or to special revelation or indeed to anything else in support of a course of action which violates a biblical principle. We cannot, whatever light we pretend to, marry an unbeliever or a man we are not prepared to obey or a woman with whom we are not prepared to have an exclusive life-long relationship. We cannot wilfully put ourselves out of a job ('he who does not provide for his own is worse than an infidel'). We cannot assume responsibilities which make it impossible for us to honour our parents or bring up our children in the knowledge and instruction of the Lord.

These things may seem obvious. But in fact many so-called problems of guidance are not problems of guidance at all. God's will is clear enough. The difficulty, for all our protests about the need for more light, is that we are not prepared to submit to it. 'I can say from experience,' wrote Donald Grey Barnhouse, 'that 95% of knowing the will of God consists in being prepared to do it before you know what it is'.

The second principle is that we are to be guided by the light of nature. This 'light of nature' is a recurring concept in the Confession and indeed would merit some study in its own right. In Chapter 1, Section 1, we are told that *the light of nature* manifests the goodness, wisdom and power of God. According to Chapter 20, the church and the civil magistrate may proceed against those who 'publish such opinions and maintain such practices as are contrary to *the light of nature*'. And Chapter 21 tells us that it is *the law of nature* that a due proportion of time be set apart for the worship of God.

The concept is also important in the New Testament. To quote only two instances: *Nature* itself teaches that it is a disgrace for a man to have long hair (1 Cor. 11: 14); and the Gentiles sometimes do by *nature* the things contained in the law (Rom. 2: 14).

Applying this to the problem of guidance, it means that we can never be 'led' to do what is unnatural: God's will will not disregard our physical needs, impose intolerable psychological stress or violate deep-seated social and sexual instincts. More important still, it means that we will not allow ourselves to fall below the world's own standards. The Gentile conscience may to a large extent be darkness, but it is still offended by a man going off with his father's wife (1 Cor. 5: 1), by religious meetings which degenerate into confused shambles (1 Cor. 14: 23), by Christians giving up their work because they think the Second Coming is imminent (2 Thess. 3: 11), by men neglecting their wives and families in the name of religion and by marriages between parties whose ages or cultures are incompatible. It is inadmissible to dismiss the judgment of such men on the ground of their being 'unspiritual'. They still have the light of nature and may be wiser, especially in practical matters, than the children of light.

Using our minds

The third principle laid down by the Confession is that
we are to be guided by Christian prudence. This roots the
task of ascertaining God's will firmly in the thinking of the
Christian. 'God's promises of guidance are not given to
save us the bother of thinking', writes John Stott. Sadly,
many Christians seem to think it is. As they plead for
guidance what they are really looking for is a way of
knowing God's will which dispenses with the need for
disciplined and rigorous thought. They not only want
absolute, revelational certainty. They want it painlessly,
in some overwhelming, supernatural flash.

The Confession, by contrast, insists on our using our
minds. This is in complete agreement with the New
Testament. 'Be transformed by the renewing of your
minds', says Paul in Rom. 12: 2, repeating the message in
Eph. 4: 23, 'Be renewed in the spirit of your minds'. Peter
is equally insistent: 'Gird up your minds', he writes (1
Peter 1: 13).

Basically, then, Christians will come to know God's will
through careful reflection. But in saying this we should
not forget that what we are talking about is *Christian*
prudence. We are not discussing the natural human mind.
We are considering the new mind of a man or woman
indwelt by the Spirit, operating prayerfully and depen-
dently and aiming for the glory of God. Such a mind will
be enriched by experience, strengthened by interaction
with other Christian minds and sensitive to every biblical
guideline, general and specific.

This sensitiveness — this spiritual fine-tuning — is of
enormous importance. If we grieve the Holy Spirit, neglect the Scriptures and cut ourselves off from Christian
fellowship, our minds will become totally unreliable. The
backslider will make monumentally wrong decisions because his prudence will no longer be Christian. It will be

worldly and selfish and lead to courses of action which, however plausible, will be totally contrary to the will of God.

If so much stress is to be laid on weighing up things for ourselves, what are the factors which, according to Scripture, we ought to be considering?

First, our own inclination. What we ourselves want can never be decisive. Neither, however, can it be ignored. When Paul lays down rules for the ordination of elders he begins by saying, 'He who desires the episcopate desires a good work' (1 Tim. 3: 1). As a general rule, if God wants us to do something He will make us want to do it. As Oliver Barclay points out, there is certainly no virtue in the idea that the most unpleasant alternative is always the right one.

Second, we will ponder all the advice we receive. Christian fellowship is about sharing: and one thing to be shared is our decision-making. There are always others older, wiser, more experienced and more objective (about our situation) than ourselves. These friends must accept the responsibility of advising. It is no help if they simply say, 'You must make up your own mind!' Of course we must: and of course it is also true that the best thing about advice is that you can refuse it. But we still need all the help we can get. In some situations, indeed, the church should make the decisions formally and officially. This was done frequently in the past. Today, the movements of ministers are too much a matter of individual whim, with far too little regard to the needs of congregations and the gifts of individuals.

Third, we must consider our own gifts. Christian service, even in the secular sphere, is determined to a large extent by the abilities God has given to us. These may be manual, artistic, professional, commercial, political or ecclesiastical. It is difficult to be realistic in judging ourselves in this connection. On the one hand, we are liable to think of ourselves more highly than we ought: on the other, we are liable to disparage ourselves. The Bible prescribes a middle course: we are to exercise sober judgment (Rom. 12: 3). In the secular sphere, the subjective element is hardly important. Examinations, interviews and other assessments will show us all too clearly where we stand and dramatically narrow our career options. But within the church, too, judgment of our gifts will often be in the hands of others and what we need is grace to submit to it. A candidate for the ministry who refuses the church's judgment shows by that very refusal that he is unfit for the office.

Fourth, we must weigh up the probable impact on our families of the various options open to us. What demands will be made on the wife? Is there a good school locally or will schooling involve the children being away from home? Is there a strong local church which will *give* rather than *require* support? Will our children find other Christians of their own age? Will they find employment? These — and many other similar factors — deserve to be pondered over and over again. Wives — and maybe even children — may have a right to volunteer for work in deprived or even dangerous or primitive areas. But husbands have no right to dictate to them: and even less to disregard their needs.

Fifth, we should look at the implications our decisions may have for the church. We are members of the body of Christ and our decision-making cannot ignore that. So far as our wisdom allows, we must do the edifying thing, refraining from what weakens and impoverishes, from what divides, from what might injure weaker brethren and from what would expose the church to the world's scorn and contempt. Nor is it enough merely to avoid harming the church. We must aim at what is positively beneficial — acquiring skills useful to the body, extending its influence, developing useful contacts and ensuring that particular congregations have an adequate supply of office-bearers, treasurers, Sunday School teachers, youth leaders and (not least) hospitable homes for informal fellowship. The conclusion that we have something to offer, something the church needs, is of course a difficult one for humility to come to. But there are occasions when we have to decide either that we are redundant in a congregation with an embarrassment of riches or that within our own limited sphere we are temporarily irreplaceable.

Conclusions

Three brief points in conclusion.

We must never absolutise our own decisions, as if they had the force of divine revelation. The man who claims, 'God put me here' is being arrogant. So is the preacher who equates his own choice of text with God's will for his congregation (on other levels, of course, he is being manipulative and exhibitionist. He wants to instil some drama into the occasion and to remind his listeners of his personal closeness to God). All we have is our own decision, in which we may be more or less confident, but which is always fallible and always liable to be falsified by events. I can never get beyond: 'This is what I think is right. So help me God.'

Again, we must recognise that the rightness or wrongness of our decisions cannot be judged by the events which immediately follow. When Jonah wrongly decided not to go to Nineveh, all at first went well with him. When Paul rightly — and against the advice of his friends — went up to Jerusalem, his decision led to bonds and imprisonment. There are still times when those fleeing from their God-given roles will meet with marvellous encouragement and coincidences. 'The devil is apparently allowed', writes Oliver Barclay, 'not only to arrange signs, but also to bring about remarkable coincidences to tempt us to evil.' And just as surely there are times when those determined to follow God's will will encounter a harrowing succession of harassments and difficulties. These are the times when we have to cling to the truth of Cowper's familiar words:

> Deep in unfathomable mines
> Of never failing skill
> He treasures up his bright designs
> And works his sovereign will.

Finally, we must develop a proper attitude to our mistakes. How many Christians get into trouble on this score, as if God would never allow His children to make mistakes! He clearly does, for His own reasons. These mistakes are not signs that we are reprobates. Nor are they unforgiveable: the blood of Christ will cover the guilt of even our most ungodly decisions. Above all, the mistakes are not irretrievable. Through our own folly, we may sometimes find ourselves where we ought not to be. The temptation will be strong to conclude that we are condemned henceforth to live lives which are sterile and useless. But it cannot be so, if God works *all* things together for good for those who love Him (Rom. 8: 28). Wherever we are, we can live meaningfully. From wherever we are, there is a road to the glory of God. 'God provides light through every one of his tunnels,' says an anonymous writer.

Even through those we should never have got into.

CHAPTER 8

The Reality of the Spirit's Ministry

It seems natural (maybe even gratifying) that the views expressed in the preceding chapters should provoke questions from concerned readers.

A *living relationship with God?*

By far the most important question raised is whether the Holy Spirit is really involved in the personal lives of believers. Does the Christian have a living relationship with God? Does the Holy Spirit deal with us directly?

The answer to these questions must be an emphatic, Yes! The Spirit's ministry is the most important reality in our lives and the New Testament proclaims it with an astonishing breadth of vocabulary.

The Holy Spirit *indwells* the believer. This scarcely requires argument. The most important thing is to note that this indwelling is not occasional and intermittent. It is permanent and continuous. He abides in us. The Christian is irreversibly a spiritual man, even when he does not behave like one. He does not become one when he has certain feelings or assurances or victories or revelations. He is one all the time.

On the face of things, the picture of a believer having his life punctuated at critical points by the Holy Spirit is a very elevated one and the view advocated in the earlier chapters appears very cold and rationalistic by contrast. But what we are pleading for is a view of the Christian life as *consistently supernatural*. As a member of the body of

Christ the life and power of the Saviour course through the believer's veins. As a branch in the vine he is never independent of the stock. He is rooted in Christ and founded on Christ and nourished by Christ. These things are true all the time, as we face temptation, responsibility and pain. They are no less true as we seek to know God's will, trying to bring together the details of our own situation and the teaching of God's word.

The Spirit *convicts of sin*. This is obviously of great importance in the early stages of our spiritual recovery. But it does not end there. When God broke David's heart he was not a young believer (Psalm 51: 8). He was a mature man of God. The same was true of Peter when, having denied His Lord, he went out and wept bitterly. David's case, in particular, shows how blind Christians can be to their own sin until the Spirit comes and drives the reality home. For many, the profoundest convictions of sin occur not at the beginning of their spiritual lives but many years later, as the Spirit leads them out of backsliding: a road which always passes through the depths.

The Spirit *leads* us, a point made clear in Rom. 8: 14, 'All who are led by the Spirit of God are sons of God'. This passage does not refer to what we commonly call guidance nor to God protecting us from the harsh realities of life. 'The end in view in the spiritual leading of which Paul speaks,' wrote B.B. Warfield, 'is not to enable us to escape the difficulties, dangers, trials or sufferings of this life, but specifically to enable us to conquer sin.' Paul relates the Spirit's leading directly to 'mortifying the deeds of the body'. The Spirit's action lies behind our hatred of sin, our hunger and thirst for righteousness and our struggle against the defects of our own personalities.

The Spirit *helps* us. This refers especially to 'our infirmities'. We ourselves are inadequate and incompetent but the Spirit supports us. The crucial thing here is that the Spirit's work is not vicarious. Just as he does not secure for us immunity from pressure so He does not carry our burdens instead of us. He carries the load *with* us, not *for* us. To what effect? With the effect that those who began by crying, 'We can't manage!' end up being 'more than conquerors'. They not only survive. They triumph, in the very context where they once thought it impossible to live an effective Christian life.

The Spirit *witnesses to our sonship*. All agree that this witness involves the 'marks of grace' in some way. But some argue that, in addition, there is an *immediate* witness of the Holy Spirit. This is misconceived. Once we accept that the witness is through Scripture and that it relates somehow to the marks of grace it can never be immediate. The Spirit's witness is not an additional tier, independent of the other two. He is a witness, using evidence, and the evidence He uses is the work of God in our own lives.

There is an interesting similarity between the Spirit's activity in bearing witness to our sonship and His activity in bearing witness to the Bible as the Word of God. According to the Westminster Confession, Scripture 'doth abundantly evidence itself to be the word of God' (I.V.). It has all the features we would expect in a divinely-inspired book: elevatedness, unity, majesty, integrity and 'many other incomparable excellencies'. Yet, despite this evidence (not only adequate but abundant), many men remain unconvinced; others never get beyond merely having a high regard for Scripture; and even believers find their assurance ebbs and flows. Evidence alone is not enough. The Holy Spirit must give that evidence cogency and He does so by influencing our hearts and minds, making them sensitive and responsive to the evidence.

It is the same with our assurance of our own sonship. The Bible does not contain an explicit statement to the effect that any of us is a child of God. It says only, 'As many as received Christ, to them He gave authority to become children of God'. The question on which we require assurance from the Holy Spirit is, Do we belong to this group? 'God's promises and oaths,' wrote Jonathan

Edwards, 'let them be as sure as they will, cannot give strong hope and comfort to any particular person any further than he can know that those promises are made to him.'

Am I one of those to whom these promises are made? If we are, then our lives will contain evidence to that effect. The teaching of George Gillespie is interesting here (*Miscellany Questions*, Chapter XXI). At one point he writes, 'To make no trial by marks, and to trust an inward testimony under the notion of the Holy Spirit's testimony, when it is without the least evidence of any true gracious mark, this way is a deluding and ensnaring of the conscience.' But at another point he puts it this way: 'All thy marks will leave thee in the dark if the Spirit of grace do not open thine eyes that thou mayest know the things which are freely given thee of God.' And he concludes: 'In the business of assurance and full persuasion, the evidence of graces and the testimony of the Spirit are two concurrent causes or helps, both of them necessary. Without the evidence of graces, it is not a safe nor a well-grounded assurance. Without the testimony of the Spirit, it is not a *plerophory* or a full assurance.'

There are 'incomparable excellencies' by which we abundantly evidence ourselves to be the children of God: we believe, we hunger and thirst after righteousness, we love the brethren, we come frankly before God in prayer. But just as the evidences of God's authorship of Scripture do not always persuade and convince, so it is in the matter of the believer's assurance of salvation. The evidence is always there. Yet a true believer 'may wait long and conflict with many difficulties, before he be partaker of it' (Westminster Confession, XVIII.III). Furthermore, 'true believers may have the assurance of their salvation divers ways shaken, diminished and intermitted' (Westminster Confession, XVIII.IV).

The difficulty is, we need more than evidence. To quote George Gillespie again: 'Marks of grace are useless, undiscernible, unsatisfactory to the deserted and overclouded soul.' We need the Holy Spirit bearing witness by and with the marks of grace. This does not mean that He guides us through a long and labyrinthine argument, checking all the links in the chain of evidence leading to assurance. The assurance may be obtained in a flash, just as a trained mind can sum up a military, medical or political situation in a flash. The important points are, first, that the Spirit never witnesses without evidence and, secondly, that evidence alone is never enough to give us 'a full assurance and infallible persuasion'.

The Spirit is also directly connected with witness in the other (and more important) sense of our witness to Christ. It was for this, in fact, that He was given: 'You will receive power and you will be witnesses to me' (Acts 1: 8). The outpouring of the Spirit turns all the Lord's people into prophets (Acts 2: 17). He alone can give us the message, the words, the courage and the wisdom to bear effective witness. We see this very clearly in Peter's Pentecost sermon, remarkable for its new depth of understanding, its striking command of language, its fearlessness and its tactfulness. In the power of the Spirit, this complete novice in public speaking delivers a message which goes right home to the consciences of his hearers and yet does not antagonise them. This is the kind of power we need if we are to re-establish the Christian cause in Britain today.

The Spirit *helps in times of crisis*. Our Lord makes this promise explicitly, relating it in the first instance to situations where Christians are on trial for their faith: 'Don't worry about what you'll say. The Holy Spirit will teach you at that very moment what you ought to say' (Luke 12: 12). This was fulfilled when Peter and John were arrested and taken before the Sanhedrin: when challenged as to their authority for preaching and healing, Peter was filled with the Spirit (Acts 4: 8). Paul had a similar experience at Paphos. When Elymas the Magician tried to prejudice the Procunsul against Christianity, Paul was filled with the Spirit and effectively nullified the sorcerer's power.

There are many situations in life for which we cannot plan and which we can never hope to handle from our own resources of skill and experience. It is pointless to worry about them. Instead, we should train ourselves to rely implicitly on God's promise that He will give us whatever we need to handle such emergencies.

Finally, the Spirit is the source of the gifts we need for Christian service. We have already discussed this aspect of New Testament teaching. The one point which needs to be emphasised again and again is our *dependentness* in all we seek to do for Christ. We can never have things under control. No ecclesiastical or religious technology can guarantee success. We cannot even rely on the general possession of gifts. There must be specific divine working at the very point at which we work. Moreover, unlike grace (*charis*) spiritual gifts (*charismata*) are not necessarily permanent. The Spirit of the Lord departed from Saul and left him destitute of the political gift he had once possessed so abundantly. The same happened to Samson, although his gift was restored for one supreme, tragic effort at the end. A minister cannot presume upon his gifts being permanent. If we grieve the Spirit or fail to 'fan our gift into flame' (2 Tim. 1: 6) our powers will be revoked and we shall find ourselves with nothing but the empty husk of office.

The Spirit's role in guidance

But what role does the Holy Spirit have in guidance, assuming that there is no longer any place for special revelation?

First of all, without the Spirit we cannot understand what Scripture teaches. In all our decision-making, we are to obey the general rules of the word (Westminster Confession, I.VI). But the Confession also tells us that the inward illumination of the Spirit is essential for under-

standing the word itself. Without this spiritual understanding, we shall twist Scripture according to our own
prejudices and end up destroying ourselves.

Second, we need the Spirit to help us evaluate situations
correctly, especially at times of crisis. This is where the
gift of wisdom comes in. Without it, we shall sum up
'according to the flesh', looking at things not from God's
side but from men's. It is no easy matter to transcend
self-interest, worldly standards and peer-group pressure
and end up with an assessment which does justice to
spiritual criteria, the perspectives of the kingdom of God
and the overriding importance of the Saviour's glory.

Third, we need the Spirit to make us willing to do God's
will. It is simplistic to assume that the problem involved in
guidance is the purely intellectual one of ascertaining what
we ought to do. Sometimes, the real struggle only begins
once God's will is known, because that will conflicts with
our own cherished prejudices and ambitions. Jonah was
left in no doubt that he should go to Nineveh. But he fled
nonetheless. This is why prayer for guidance must always
involve not only prayer for light but prayer for willingness
to follow the light.

But all this falls short of the Spirit's giving us special,
direct revelation and many Christians find this disturbing.
So far as they are concerned, to deny immediate, personal
guidance is to deny the reality of experiential religion
itself.

Historical bearings

Let's get our historical bearings, however. This mystical view of guidance may now be virtually universal among
Christians. But it was not always so. The Westminster
Confession, for example, states categorically that 'those
former ways of God's revealing His will unto his people
have now ceased' (Westminster Confession, I.I). Later, it
asserts the perfection of Scripture: 'The whole counsel of
God, concerning all things necessary for man's salvation,

faith and life is either expressly set down in Scripture, or by good and necessary consequence, may be deduced from Scripture' (I.VI). It then adds, on the basis of this perfection, that nothing is to be added to Scripture, 'whether by *new revelations of the Spirit* or traditions of men'. Whether the Confession is right or wrong, these words show very clearly that the classic theology of the seventeenth century regarded any claims to additional revelations as inconsistent with the sufficiency and finality of Scripture.

In the last 150 years, the Confession's position has been largely discarded. Swedenborg and Joseph Smith, the founders of great modern sects, both claimed to have had special revelations. Pentecostal 'prophets' claim to receive them continually. And even Dr John Kennedy's *Days of the Fathers in Ross-shire* portrays (and commends) a mystical experientialism which it would be very difficult to reconcile with the teaching of the Confession.

But there have been other voices. Professor John Murray, for example, writes: 'The Word of God is a perfect and sufficient rule of practice. The corollary of this is that we may not look for, depend upon or demand new revelations of the Spirit.' He goes on to speak of 'the error of thinking that while the Holy Spirit does not provide us with special revelations in the form of words or visions or dreams, yet He may and does provide us with some direct feeling or impression or conviction which we are to regard as the Holy Spirit's intimation to us of what His mind and will is in our particular situation'.

Professor Paul Woolley shared Professor Murray's view. There is, he says, one very important consequence of the sufficiency of Scripture: 'God does not today guide people directly without using the Scriptures. There are no divinely given "hunches". God does not give people direct mental impressions to do this or that. People do not hear God's voice speaking within them. There is no immediate and direct unwritten communication between God and the individual human being. If the Scriptures are actually sufficient, such communication is unnecessary. On the other hand, if such communications were actually being made, every Christian would be a potential author of Scripture.'

It is important to notice what exactly it is that evangelicals regard as revelation. When the Confession says that 'those former ways of God's revealing himself have now ceased' it is referring to theophanies, dreams, visions, prophetic utterances and apostolic tradition. When evangelicals today claim direct revelation they are not thinking of any of these. They are thinking of states of consciousness, of complexes of feelings, which, they say, indicate the will of God. The mental impression itself is the revelation of what God wants them to do. A proposed sermon or a proposed move or a proposed resignation *feels* good. There is nothing wrong with having such feelings nor indeed with acting upon them. As Professor Murray points out, we must not let ourselves be trapped into the view that 'a strong or overwhelming feeling or impression or conviction is necessarily irrational or mystical.' Because our minds are limited this may be the way that all the relevant considerations focus themselves in our consciousness. But it remains only a feeling or impression nonetheless. Even when it is absolutely right it is not a revelation. A man who says that one plus one equals two will have an overwhelming impression that he is saying exactly the right thing. But then so will some who say the earth is flat. The correctness of their respective convictions cannot be decided by the way they feel about them.

Guidance in the early church

Behind the idea that believers are still guided by direct revelation there appears to lie the assumption that whatever people enjoyed during the apostolic period we ought to enjoy today. But if we look closely we find that in those early days things were not exactly as we suppose.

For one thing, the very reason why there had to be prophets and apostles in the early church was precisely that all believers did not enjoy special revelation. Men like Agabus were needed both because there was no completed canon and because the Spirit's ministry, intimate and decisive though it was, left large areas of uncertainty.

It is intriguing, too, that at critical moments in the church's development no special divine guidance was given. In Acts 1: 21-26, for example, when the disciples decided to appoint a successor to Judas, there is no revelation. They have to resort to a lot: and it is far from clear that God's will was expressed in the lot (except in the general sense that the fall of the dice always lies within the divine decree). We certainly hear no more of Matthias.

We find the same thing in connection with the appointment of the Seven in Acts 6: 1-6. The decision marked a major step forward in the organisation of the church. But it was prompted by a simple emergency arising out of the Hellenists' complaints that their widows were being neglected. Throughout, the church's leaders are guided by nothing more than 'the light of nature and Christian prudence'. They argue, simply, that it is inappropriate for them to waste their time in administration, that the tasks must devolve upon others and that those appointed must be men full of the Holy Spirit and of wisdom. The final decision is taken on the basis that the proposal 'pleased the whole multitude'.

When Paul arranges for the appointment of elders in Galatia (Acts 14: 23) they are appointed by popular election: and when Titus appoints them in Crete he is directed to look out for certain qualities and base his decision on these (Titus 1: 5-9).

It is surely significant that in such an obviously charismatic community as the early church decision-making should so often have been a matter of mere common sense.

It is more fascinating still to notice that even when specific divine guidance was given the details were left to be worked out according to the judgment of the people involved. The commissioning of Saul and Barnabas is indeed a matter of direct revelation, which is hardly surprising considering that it marks the effective beginning of the Gentile mission. But once the missionaries are ordained, all the evidence suggests that they have to work out the details for themselves: what towns to visit, whom to take with them, how to travel, how long to stay. As they take these decisions, they are, of course, Spirit-filled men, but there is little hint of special revelations and none at all of an inclination to regard their own feelings as synonymous with the will of God. All the ordinary problems of missionaries are there, even the bitter blow of John Mark abandoning them at Pamphylia.

The same situation is repeated in Acts 16. They are forbidden by the Spirit to preach the word in Asia. They then, most humanly, attempt to go to Bithynia, but are again frustrated: whereupon they make their own decision to go to Troas. At Troas, Paul receives the vision (not a mental impression) of the man from Macedonia: 'Come over and help us!' High drama! But from then on the story is a mundane one of sailing to Samothrace, thence to Neapolis and finally to Phillipi. Once at Phillipi, they decide (without any revelation) to go down to the riverside on the Sabbath Day. As a result of that decision, Lydia is converted. But when, without any direct guidance, Paul rebukes the demon-possessed girl, apparent disaster follows. They are imprisoned and eventually expelled.

Paul's visit to Athens brings out the same principles. It is no revelation that brings him there: merely the fact that that is where he is escorted by the brethren from Berea (Acts 17: 15). At Athens, he preaches his great sermon before the Areopagus: not, however, because some message is 'given' to him but because his soul is provoked by the idolatry and superstition he sees all around him. The sermon itself is a model of the judicious application of biblical truth to a particular, and even peculiar, audience.

Remarkable stories

The argument we have put forward in this chapter is often countered by anecdote. Everyone knows remarkable stories of men and women who had an overwhelming sense that they must follow a certain course of action. They obeyed the feeling and the outcome vindicated them gloriously.

It is dangerous to allow theology to be guided by extra-biblical narrative. But allowing the relevance of such incidents for the moment, it is surely clear that they could be paralleled many times from non-Christian sources. Every detective has hunches: and Winston Churchill had an overwhelming sense that he was on the right course when he wrote in 1939, 'I felt as if I were walking with destiny, and that all my past life had been a preparation for this hour and this trial.' Furthermore, for every hunch which turns out to be correct there are many more which do not. 'That people have hunches is obvious,' writes Paul Woolley: 'That many of them work out very well and others quite poorly is also obvious.' But only the successful ones are related.

Then there is M'Cheyne's advice: 'Get your text, your thoughts, your words from God'. This may not be as harmless as it looks. When is the preacher's word from God? As far as we are concerned, whenever it is based four-square on Scripture. How we feel in relation to it is immaterial. We certainly need wisdom to decide which part of Scripture to expound in a given situation. In fact, the possession of such wisdom is an indispensable part of the call to preach. But even when our judgment falters, God's word remains God's word, deserving reverent exposition and responsive hearing. The authority lies in the Scriptures themselves, not in our mental impressions.

But have we ourselves not known situations where we were sure God had *given* us the word? No, because before we ever began to preach we had come to hold the very opinions on this subject which we hold today. But what we have known is this: A fair measure of confidence that we had prepared something we could preach *with liberty*. We could sleep well the night before. But as often as not (indeed, more often than not) the thing didn't work and it was agony to deliver. On other occasions, we have had the opposite experience: a sermon in which we had no confidence and a night without sleep. But when the day came, it worked, at least to the extent that the actual preaching of it was an enjoyable and even an exhilarating experience.

The feelings we have before preaching and feelings we have during preaching are not important, except to ourselves. What matters is the truth of what we preach: and what we should pray for is not assurance before we preach it or liberty as we preach it but wisdom and courage to declare the whole counsel of God.

The place of the mind

Let us not forget that the church still enjoys revelation. The Bible is the living word of God, still giving us abundant and clear guidance. But when it comes to deciding how to get from Edinburgh to Bombay we are in the same position as Paul seeking to get from Troas to Samothrace. We have to think. In fact, it is quite astonishing how much emphasis the Bible places on the role of the mind in the Christian life. We are to be transformed through the renewing of our minds (Rom. 12: 2). We are to gird up the loins of our minds (1 Peter 1: 13). We serve the law of God with our minds (Rom. 7: 25). We are to be renewed in the spirit of our minds (Eph. 4: 23). Obviously it is not in the abandonment of the intellect that we are to serve God but in its consecration and application. Coming back to the model with which we began: we are to *think* what Christ *thought*.

That intellect itself, as we have emphasised repeatedly, is not ordinary. It is indwelt by the Spirit and doesn't think or judge in the same way as the intellect of a natural man. But the newness of the regenerate intellect is not the only charismatic element in the Christian's decision-making. We must also reckon with the gift of wisdom: 'If any of you lacks wisdom, let him ask it of God' (James 1: 5). This is more than common sense and more even than the day-to-day insight of the born-again man. It is a special *charisma*, enabling men like Solomon and Stephen to lead the church and to solve the problems which arise in counselling and administration. It does not involve God *revealing* solutions to us but it probably does involve an instinctive knowledge of the right thing to do. The gift is available to all of us and as we look at the intractable problems facing both church and society we should be more and more conscious that nothing short of supernatural sagacity will meet our need.

Many people will say that the line we have taken on this subject is discouraging, because it calls in question the experience of many of God's people. To that, we can say only one thing: Think how discouraged many ordinary Christians become when they hear others talking of these marvellous experiences which they themselves have never had. Our own reflections arose, many years ago, precisely out of such discouragements. It was a mighty uplift then to find that we were not alone in our deprivation. If anything we have said helps someone else to accept himself before God, despite lacking voices, visions and overwhelming certainties, we shall be happy.

CHAPTER 9

Go on being filled!

The preceding chapters left much unsaid, especially on the positive side. It would be most unfortunate to give the impression that our experience of the Holy Spirit is any less urgent or less vivid today than it was in the days of the apostles. In fact, the New Testament is full of clear directions on the subject of establishing and maintaining a close relationship with the Holy Spirit.

Of these, the most comprehensive is probably the one given in Eph. 5: 18, *Be filled with* (or *in*) *the Spirit*. This is one of a series of basic principles of conduct laid down by the apostle as a sequel to the great doctrinal statements of the earlier part of the epistle. In 4: 1, he urges us to walk worthy of the vocation with which we were called. In 4: 17, he exhorts us not to walk as the other Gentiles walk. In 5: 1, he directs us to be imitators of God, as dear children. The principle laid down in 5: 18 belongs to the same order of thought. Being filled with the Spirit is related not to the realm of euphoric experience but to the ethical rigours of the Christian life.

Misunderstanding

It is important to guard Paul's language here against misunderstanding.

For example, he is not asking them to experience something they have not experienced before. It is clear from Acts 19: 1-7 that the Ephesian believers had already received the Holy Spirit. The same thing is made abundantly plain in Eph. 1: 13f., 'You were sealed with the Holy Spirit of the promise.' In fact, as we saw in a previous chapter, the New Testament knows nothing of believers who have not received the Spirit, been baptised in the

Spirit and been filled with the Spirit. The pattern set in
Acts (1: 4f., 1: 8, 2: 4 and 2: 38) is that this great initiatory
experience of the Holy Spirit is part of the very meaning of
being a Christian. What Paul is referring to in Eph. 5: 18 is
an experience they have all had already, but which he
wants them, in some sense, to have again.

Equally important, however, Paul is not referring to a
single, definitive experience. The tense he uses is the
present continuous: *Go on being filled*. He is not describing
something which happens only once but telling us that we
not only may, but must, be filled many times over.

One further negative: Eph. 5: 18 is not interested so
much in an experience as in a duty. Its thrust is not that we
should wait passively for God to do something to us but
that there is something we must do for ourselves. Nor is
this passage exceptional in this respect. In a more sustained way, Paul makes the same point in Galatians 5:
16ff. We are to *walk (about)* by the Spirit, *live* for the Spirit
and *march* in step with the Spirit. The same emphasis on
obligation is found in Eph. 4: 30, 'Grieve not the Holy
Spirit of God.' All of these are salutary reminders that our
relationship with the Holy Spirit is not an inert one.
Where a Christian lacks spirituality, the reason lies not in
some sovereign divine decision but in our personal failure
to take the measures prescribed in Scripture for maintaining a living relationship with God.

Filling someone already full

But how can a person who has already been filled in the
Spirit be filled again? How can a person who is full keep on
being filled?

Part of the answer lies in the experience of Peter described in Acts 4: 8. He had already been filled on the Day
of Pentecost. Yet here he is, a few days later, being filled
again. This latter experience is clearly related to the
Lord's promise in Luke 12: 11ff.: 'When they bring you
before magistrates, take no thought how or what you shall

answer: for the Holy Spirit will teach you in that very hour what you ought to say.' Peter is facing a crisis: and he received a special filling of the Spirit to deal with it. The same thing happened to Paul in Paphos (Acts 13: 9). Elymas the Sorcerer was trying to dissuade the proconsul, Sergius Paulus, from becoming a Christian. Paul was filled with the Spirit and delivered a rebuke so solemn and so effective that the proconsul, 'when he saw what was done, believed, being astonished at the doctrine of the Lord.'

What is being taught here, surely, is that if we venture forth in humble dependence on the Spirit of God, He will enable us to cope with any emergency. We cannot simply rely on past experiences. Every crisis creates its own need and the Spirit meets that need, filling us time after time as we are challenged for our faith, overwhelmed with responsibility or faced with special temptations.

Further light is shed on the problem in the description of Stephen given in Acts 6: 5. He was a man 'full of faith and of the Holy Spirit.' This is not a description of something instantaneous and momentary but of an abiding condition. Here is a man who never lapsed, who never declined, who never fell away. He remained, habitually, full of the Spirit. His whole character — his relationships, his emotions, his ambitions, his reactions — remained under the Spirit's control. That is the Christian ideal and it cannot be secured by any single experience. It can be secured only by an unending succession of replenishments, very much along the lines suggested in John 1: 16, 'From his fulness have we all received, grace upon grace.'

The Lord's words in Mt. 7: 7ff. are also relevant: 'Ask and it shall be given to you; seek, and ye shall find; knock, and it shall be opened unto you.' These words are not addressed to the unconverted. In their original setting they have nothing to do with a man seeking Christ for the first time. They have to do with established Christians seeking the Holy Spirit: 'If ye, then, being evil, know how to give good gifts unto your children how much more shall your heavenly Father give the Holy Spirit to them that ask him?' These people are already saved. They are already Christians. They already have the Spirit. Yet they are to ask for Him. They are to seek Him. And they are to do so with all the earnestness and importunity of a child seeking food. The Holy Spirit is not something God's children can do without. He is indispensable. Nor is He something they can store up. They need more and more. They need again and again. And the only way they can ensure that they are always full is to be always asking.

The same point is made in a slightly different way in John 15: 4, 'Abide in me.' The background to that, surely, is a distinction between *being in Christ* (or *coming to be in Christ*) and *abiding in Christ*. The initial acceptance of the Saviour and commitment to Him are obviously indispensable. But they need to be re-enacted, repeatedly and continuously. The cross is taken up not simply once for all, but daily. There is an analogy here with the life of Christ Himself. He not only made the decision to become man but, as man, 'humbled himself', going down further and further into the abyss of nothingness. Spiritual fruitfulness is not the result of merely coming to Christ. It is the result of adhering — of clinging — to Him by faith and prayer. The original context of the Lord's words was the metaphor of the vine and the branches: 'As the branch cannot bear fruit of itself, unless it abides in the vine, no more can you unless you abide in me.' There must be a permanently close bond between graft and stock if the sap is to flow freely.

The signs

What are the signs of a Spirit-filled man? The context of Ephesians 5: 18 indicates two things.

First, the results are at the furthest possible remove from the symptoms of intoxication: 'Be not drunk with wine wherein is excess, but . . .' The two experiences are

sharply contrasted. Intoxication leads to extravagant behaviour, to the loss of self-control and to exaggerated
self-confidence. Being filled with the Spirit does not. The
charge that the disciples at Pentecost were drunk was
purely malicious. All the signs are that they were totally
self-possessed, proclaiming the wonderful works of God
and (in Peter's case) able to react at once to the taunts of
the multitude by preaching an evangelistic sermon which
was a model of insight, courage and wisdom. There were
clearly those in the New Testament church who claimed
that the experience of the Holy Spirit led to ecstasy and to
a loss of self-control. Paul repudiates this in 1 Cor. 14: 32:
'The spirits of the prophets are subject to the prophets.'

There is nothing at all destructive in the experience of
the Holy Spirit and Christians should be exceedingly
careful lest the language they use give any impression to
the contrary. It is utterly misleading to speak of men and
women as God-intoxicated or Spirit-intoxicated, as if the
acme of spirituality were that men lose their inhibitions,
their self-consciousness and their self-control and man-
ifest their 'liveliness' by swooning, chanting, clapping and
stamping their feet. Such thinking has lost all connection
with Scripture, which expects us to present our bodies to
God in *reasonable* service, to behave with decency and
order and to practise a love which is always aware of other
people and their needs. Far from over-riding men's capa-
bilities, the filling of the Spirit sharpens our minds,
strengthens our self-control and disciplines our emotions.
The very last thing it does is to unfit us for life in this
perplexing and bemusing world.

Second, Holy Spirit baptism leads to the great moral
and spiritual features which Paul goes on to describe in
Eph. 5: 18-6: 9.

That means, to begin with, that the Spirit-filled man
sings and makes melody in his heart. Such singing, says
Paul, is directed specifically to the Lord. It is doxological.
The man who is having this experience spends his life

saying, 'Unto him be glory in the church through Christ
Jesus, world without end.' We are back again in the very
atmosphere of Pentecost, where men were heard proclaiming the mighty acts of God. They are not singing mere
ditties or singing simply for the sake of self-expression.
The joy in their hearts finds an outlet in spiritual songs
(songs inspired by the Spirit and having the things of the
Spirit for their theme). Furthermore, the songs and the
singing are aimed at others: 'speaking to one another.' In a
parallel passage in Colossians (3: 16) Paul puts it even
more strongly: they are to teach and admonish one
another. Even in the singing of spiritual men there is
doctrine and admonition. There is a concern to edify
others.

What Paul is saying here should be compared with Ps.
40: 3: 'He hath put a new song in my mouth, even praise to
our God: the many shall see and fear and shall trust in the
Lord.' Not only is there melody in his heart. There is a
song on his lips; and that song is directed not only to God,
but to men. What the psalm brings out so beautifully is
that the men aimed at are not God's men or believing men.
They are 'the many' — the *Rabim* — the unbelieving
Gentiles. The spiritual man (just as at Pentecost) wants the
world to hear his song: and, at last, to sing his song.

Again, being filled with the Spirit leads to gratitude:
'giving thanks always and in all things.' The striking thing
in Paul's expression here is its comprehensiveness. The
Spirit-filled man can give thanks always! and in all things!
There is a marvellous progression in the biblical teaching
on this whole question of our ability to cope with changing
circumstances. In Psalm 23, we find God's flock moving
fearlessly through the valley of the shadow of death, 'for
thou art with me.' In Job 1: 21, the patriarch accepts
personal tragedy with quiet resignation: 'The Lord gave
and the Lord hath taken away. Blessed be the name of the
Lord.' In Phil. 4: 11, we hear Paul's great statement, 'I
have learned, in whatsoever state I am, therewith to be

content.' What spiritual strength that shows! Jailed, chained to a soldier, cold, hungry and hearing nothing but bad news about his beloved churches. And yet, content! But the vision in Eph. 5: 20 is more awesome still. Not only fearless, not only resigned, not only content, but positively thankful — always! and in all things! whatever kind of day he is having! whatever things he is experiencing!

Here again is something we find in the psalms, written at a far earlier stage of revelation and yet reflecting an equally clear experience of both adversity and grace. 'Every day will I bless thee and praise thy name time without end' (Ps. 145: 2). Every day! Days when there are enemies or bereavement or pain or peril or persecution or disappointment or isolation. Every day! Every single day! There is surely nothing greater in the whole Christian life than this triumph of the humble soul over adversity in all its forms. More than any intensity of emotion, more than any eminence in gifts, more than any public usefulness, it is the hall-mark of a spiritual man.

Yet again, the filling of the Spirit shows itself in relationships. This is what Paul develops in Eph. 5: 21-6: 9, showing the implication of the Spirit's filling for husbands and wives, parents and children, masters and servants. The key-word is *submission*: 'Submit yourselves to one another in the fear of God.' He does not mean, of course, servile acquiescence in one another's orders, but the constant willingness to submit our own interests to those of others. In fact, he is calling us back to the mind of Christ, who, as we are told in Phil. 2: 5, looked not on his own things but on the things of others. The very reason that He made Himself nothing was that He put others before Himself. The same *motif* is evident in Eph. 5: 22 ff., where Paul makes Christ's treatment of His church the model for Christian marriage. Here again the teaching is awe-inspiring in its ethical rigour. The Spirit-filled man treats His wife the way Christ treated the church. The

Spirit-filled man treats His children the way God treats
His children. The Spirit-filled man treats His servants the
way God treats His servants. He cannot use his religion as
a pretext for inhumanity or use the claims of God to excuse
arrogance or discourtesy. If a man is filled with the Spirit,
he is meticulously careful in his personal relationships.

Maybe the outstanding feature of Paul's discussion of
this topic is that he says nothing at all about *rights*: not
husbands' rights or wives' rights or parents' rights or
children's rights or masters' rights or servants' rights. All
the emphasis falls on *duties*. The Spirit-filled man is not
interested in his rights. His concern is with his responsibilities and obligations. What other men owe him does not
matter. What does matter is that he himself should dis-
charge what he owes to other men.

Explaining our Experiences

This doctrine, if we have understood it correctly, helps
us understand two common features of the spiritual life.

First, it explains the fact that many Christians, long
after their conversions, have had unforgettable spiritual
experiences. Some have had their hearts flooded with
assurance. Some have been given an overwhelming sense
of the beauty of God. Some have received new spiritual
strength which has transformed their ministries. Such
experiences are often referred to today as Holy Spirit
baptisms or Holy Spirit sealings. We would deny that. But
we would not deny the experiences themselves. It is only
the labels that are wrong. There is nothing in the experience of men like Rutherford, Flavell or Edwards but what
the teaching of Eph. 5: 18 would lead us to expect. For
every Christian, there is indeed a great, definitive filling at
the time of conversion. But that leaves room for many
more fillings, depending on our own spiritual hunger, the
crises we face and the responsibilities we bear. Our Christian lives are made up of new beginnings and these are often
more vivid and traumatic than our original conversions.

But Paul's language in Eph. 5: 18 also explains something else: the low level of spiritual attainment in many Christian lives. Some Christians simply don't grow. They remain spiritual babes, immature, ignorant and worldly. Others make some initial progress and then stagnate. Their early promise is never realised.

These facts are often used as conclusive proof against the doctrine that all Christians have received Holy Spirit baptism. The argument is a simple one: 'Look at that man! He's a Christian. But see how immature and worldly he is. Can you really believe that he has received the baptism in the Holy Spirit?'

But the argument proves too much. One could say with equal force: 'Can you really believe that that man is born again? That he is a new creature? That he is united to Christ?' The real reason for some disciples being only shadows of what Christians ought to be is not that they lack baptism in the Holy Spirit but that they are not heeding Paul's instruction in Eph. 5: 18: 'Go on being filled with the Spirit!' God has withheld nothing from them. But they are never at His door asking for more.

CHAPTER 10

Can we be Reformed Pentecostals?

Many voices are telling us today that it is time for the Reformed and the Pentecostal churches to lay aside their differences and come together. In his foreword to Dr Lloyd-Jones' *Joy Unspeakable* the Reverend Peter Lewis, for example, suggests that 'for many reasons — biblical, historical and experiential — it is becoming increasingly untenable and even absurd to see these two movements as fundamentally alien to one another.' As Mr Lewis sees things, Pentecostalism is totally compatible with the Reformed tradition.

Much to learn

How much of this can we concede? There is no doubt that the two traditions have much to learn from each other, although to some extent Mr Lewis is working with stereotypes. Not all Pentecostal churches have been weak on doctrine and certainly many of the Reformed churches we know belie the description, 'replete with sound doctrine but cramped in regard to experience and assurance'. Nevertheless, we could learn much from Pentecostals in terms of zeal, mobilisation of the whole body of believers and longing for the Spirit's ministry. But then, we could also learn much from Roman Catholicism, Liberalism and the Theology of Liberation. All Christian traditions have much to learn from each other. But that does not justify their merging.

It is quite possible, too, for an individual or a church to believe firmly in the Five Points of Calvinism and at the same time to believe in the subsequence of Holy Spirit baptism and in the continuance of tongue-speaking. Such churches, if they conform to Mr Lewis' blue-print, will have regular expository preaching, modern hymns, informal worship and an aversion to all things Victorian.

But the question is, Are the two theologies fundamentally compatible? There are at least two areas of tension, both involving major watch-words of the Reformation: *Sola scriptura* (Scripture alone) and *sola fide* (by faith alone).

Sola scriptura

First, *sola scriptura*. According to historic Reformed theology the church is taught and governed by the word of God given through apostles and prophets and set down in Holy Scripture. The scripture is not only the supreme standard. It is the only standard. Furthermore, once the last book of the New Testament came to be written, this revelation was perfect and sufficient: 'The whole counsel of God, concerning all things necessary for his own glory, man's salvation, faith and life is either expressly set down in scripture, or by good and necessary consequence may be deduced from Scripture' (Westminster Confession, Chapter I. VI). Consequently, nothing is ever to be added to the Scripture, 'whether by new revelations of the Spirit or traditions of men' (*ibid*).

In Pentecostalism, this doctrine is under attack from several different directions, not least from the ministry of alleged prophets. Indeed, this is one of the proudest boasts of the Charismatic churches; the voice of prophecy has been restored. But the precise meaning of what is claimed is far from clear. To most ordinary Christians *prophesying* means *foretelling*. Charismatics play down this element, with some justification. The oft-repeated claim of biblical scholars that prophecy is not *foretelling* but *forthtelling* may be a cliché, but it is true nonetheless. This becomes clear immediately we remember that the greatest of the prophets was Moses, who certainly did not major on prediction but on *torah* (instruction). On the other hand, prediction was a prominent element in biblical prophecy, even in the New Testament. Agabus, for example, foretold that the Jews would arrest Paul and deliver him to the Gentiles (Acts 21: 11). The Revelation of John ('the words of the prophecy of this book') speaks of 'things which must shortly be done' (Rev. 1: 1). It is interesting, too, that in the Old Testament, the test of a prophet was whether his predictions came true: 'When a prophet speaketh in the name of the Lord, if the thing follow not nor come to pass, that is the thing which the Lord hath not spoken, but the prophet hath spoken it presumptuously' (Deut. 18: 22). Furthermore, if a prophet spoke falsely, he was to be put to death: 'The prophet which shall presume to speak in my name a word which I have not commanded him to speak, even that prophet shall die' (Deut. 18: 20). Are these principles applied in Pentecostal assemblies today? All their prophets make predictions, but by no means all come true. What happens? Are such prophets stoned? If not, what has happened to the claim that we are returning exactly to the primitive biblical situation? If false prophets are not stoned then Pentecostals, too, are conceding some kind of transitionalism. Some parts of the Bible are no longer binding. In words they are so fond of applying to others, they are taking scissors to the Bible.

They also insist that their prophesying is not an addition to Scripture. It is not canonical. But the meaning of this, too, is obscure. Some genuine prophecy certainly was non-canonical in the sense that it was never recorded in writing with a view to being incorporated in the authoritative books of the Christian church. Pentecostals may be saying something like this. They have no desire that their prophecies be treated as holy writings. But they seem to be saying more: that there were two kinds of prophecy, the one revelational and normative, the other informal and hortatory. On the one hand, there is classical biblical prophecy; on the other, there are exhortations and directions relating to particular, passing situations.

The difficulty with this is that such a notion of prophecy finds little support in Scripture. There may be some room for it in Numbers 11: 29, 'Would that all the Lord's people were prophets.' But this may be no more than a longing on Moses' part and it may never have found fulfilment. Acts 2: 17 may also suggest a more general sense of prophecy. It sees Pentecost as a fulfilment of Joel 2: 28: ' I will pour out my Spirit upon all flesh; and your sons and your daughters shall prophesy, your old men shall dream dreams, your young men shall see visions.' It can be argued from this that in the new dispensation all the people of God (sons, daughters, old men, young men) are to be prophets and indeed that this is why the baptism of the Spirit was given: 'You shall receive power and you shall be witnesses to me' (Acts 1: 8). This would agree with the vision of Jeremiah 31: 31-34: 'I will make a new covenant with the house of Israel and with the house of Judah. I will put my law in their inward parts and write it in their hearts. And they shall teach no more every man his neighbour and every man his brother, saying, Know the Lord: for they shall all know me, from the least of them unto the greatest of them, saith the Lord.' If these passages point to prophecy as universal, then the meaning of prophecy itself must be reduced accordingly. The prophet is the witness who proclaims the virtues of the One who called him from darkness into His own marvellous light (1 Pet. 2: 9). This is not at all to be despised nor dismissed as non-charismatic. It is supremely charismatic. The very purpose for which the Spirit was given was to enable the church to bear witness to Christ. But then, if this is all we mean by prophecy charismatic assemblies and charismatic prophets are nothing special. All Christians are prophets and all churches are prophetic.

But the word prophecy is seldom, if ever, used in the New Testament in this sense. Two whole pages in Strong's *Exhaustive Concordance* are devoted to *prophesy* and its cognates and in every instance (with the possible exception of Acts 2: 17) it has its usual, specialised meaning. To be a prophet in the New Testament church is to occupy a position second only to an apostle; to prophesy is to make an authoritative disclosure of God's will. And this is really what is being claimed by the new prophets. Why otherwise the constant appeals to the example of the New Testament prophets, the Montanists and the Irving-ites? Whether foretelling or forthtelling, today's seers are making authoritative canonical pronouncements. They are declaring what the Spirit has told them: and what the Spirit says cannot be non-canonical. If a prophet directs a young couple to the mission-field, to the mission-field they must go. If he prescribes a certain course of action for the congregation, then the congregation must comply. If this is not an alternative canon, it is certainly an enlarged one, implying that Scripture itself is not sufficient. For faith, life and salvation today we need more: and there is no shortage of voices offering to supply it. To some, this is an entirely welcome development, offering more informa-tion and greater light and certainty for the church. But the results are calamitous, especially in the area of Christian freedom. One of the greatest affirmations of the Reforma-tion was that 'God alone is Lord of the conscience and hath left it free from the doctrines and commandments of men' (Westminster Confession, Chapter XX. II). Today, the commandments of pretended 'shepherds' are invading the most private and personal areas of many Christian lives as the tyranny of the mediaeval church is replaced by a tyranny of new seers, claiming a submission that flouts every New Testament principle of service and *kenosis*.

Exclusion of Scripture from key areas

But the authority of Scripture is under pressure at another point, too. It is being excluded from key areas of the Christian life. The Reformers' approach to worship, for example, was governed by the Puritan principle:

Nothing was to be imposed on the worshipping congregation unless it was sanctioned by Scripture. They may have been wrong to have espoused such a principle. But espouse it they did. Furthermore, they regarded it as crucial. Indeed, this is what Puritanism was all about. There could be no bishops, no altars, no incense, no vestments, no Prayer Book because there was no authority for such things in the word of God. Today, however, people claiming to be Reformed and even to be Puritans want to introduce ballet, mime and drama into the church's worship. People who claim to be calling us back to primitive, apostolic Christianity are creating a new ecclesiastical office: choreographer. It does not occur to such men to ask, Is there divine authority for this? Far less do they think of asking, On what plane does worship operate? Is it on the horizontal (what people like) or on the vertical (what is well-pleasing to God)? Our plays, mimes and dramas may be very enjoyable and even deeply moving. But have we any reason whatever to think that God wants them and is pleased with them?

Behind these new trends there appears to lie a misunderstanding of the New Testament accounts of the life of the early church and particularly of First Corinthians Fourteen. We seem to have concluded that the early Christian gatherings were marked by great jollity, lots of physical movement, uninhibited self-expression and above all lots and lots of music. But how sound is such a conclusion?

We certainly do not lack materials for an answer. We have a great summary account of these early gatherings in Acts 2: 42. They had four outstanding features: teaching, fellowship, breaking bread and prayers. We have an account of an early prayer-meeting in Acts 4: 23ff., a report of God's judgment on unacceptable behaviour in Acts 5: 1-11, a description of a leaders' meeting in Acts 15: 6-29, a glimpse into a late-night meeting in Acts 20: 7-12 and a record of a poignant farewell in Acts 20: 17-38.

These passages may not tell us all we would like to know but certain facts stand out very clearly. For example, the early church was not a particularly musical church. There is no reference in these passages to any kind of musical instrument and even the references to singing are scanty. This is in marked contrast to the church today. Christians seem to share to the full the current addiction to background noise. Music, it seems, is next to godliness and indispensable to any Christian gathering. Indeed, to many Christians it is the decisive criterion when it comes to choosing a church.

Furthermore, the gatherings of the early church were firmly structured. Disorder and confusion were specifically condemned (1 Cor. 14: 33). Everything was to be decent and orderly. Clear guidance was given as to how, for example, the Lord's Supper was to be administered. Charismatic activity, too, was carefully regulated. No more than two (or at the most, three) people were to speak in tongues at any one meeting: and none at all were to speak if there were no interpreter present. Prophets were to speak in turn and to give way to one another. Surprisingly, too, very detailed instructions were given as to the behaviour of women. They were not to speak, they were not to teach and even when it came to praying, Paul laid the responsibility on the men: 'I desire that the men pray in every place' (1 Timothy 2: 8). Even in the matter of dress there are firm stipulations: 'women are to adorn themselves in modest apparel, with shamefastness and sobriety.' There is to be no braided (plaited) hair, no gold jewellery, no expensive clothes. It would be perilous to interpret these instructions legalistically but even if we confine ourselves to their spirit, they are obviously calling for restraint.

In fact, this is the tone of all the clues we have as to the structure of these New Testament meetings. The spontaneity was certainly not unlimited. No doubt, like their counterparts today many tongue-speakers and prophets must have felt 'led' to speak when 'the rules' forbade it. No doubt, too, many women 'felt called' to teach and to preach (especially when they heard the men doing it so badly). But they had to respect the order. In these apostolic directions, just as much as in the deepest doctrines, they met 'the mind of Christ' (1 Cor. 14: 37) and no matter how deep the inward compulsion, the spirit of the prophets was to be subject to the prophets (1 Cor. 14: 32).

Emotional temperature

Nor was the emotional temperature of these early Christian meetings exactly as Charismatics imagine. Certainly there was joy and doxology. But as early as Acts 2: 43 we read that, 'Fear came on every soul'. It is interesting that this comes immediately after the words, 'They continued in the apostles' teaching, in fellowship, in the breaking of bread and in prayers.' We find the same thing in Acts 5: 11: 'And great fear came upon all the church and upon as many as heard these things.' Even in 1 Cor. 14: 24, 25, this note is sounded: a stranger walking into the assembly is going to be convicted, fall down on his face and worship and confess that God really is among these Christians. In fact these words highlight the key issue: the presence of God in the Christian gatherings. The fear of Acts 2: 43 is directly linked with Pentecost, in which the church experienced the *parousia* of the Holy Spirit and became the temple of the living God. This is even more obvious in Acts 5: 11 where the fear is the direct result of the death of Ananias and Sapphira; a death which was itself due to their not reckoning seriously with the implications of God's presence in the church. They thought they could sin with impunity. Instead, they experienced the presence of God as a consuming fire.

What we have to remember is that the transition from the Old Testament to the New did not involve any lowering in the level of religious seriousness. Under the Old Testament it was not easy for the church to live with God.

The presence of God was, at the merely human level, a nuisance. The law was so pervasive and the divine presence so obtrusive that Israel could never relax like the other nations. It was like having the Admiral always aboard the ship. The New Testament did not eliminate this. It intensified it. There was a new form of the presence, namely, the *parousia* and indwelling of the Spirit, and this was not in the least lower or less demanding: 'If you call on Him as Father, who judges every man impartially according to his works, pass the time of your sojourning here in fear' (1 Pet. 1: 17).

No man in our generation had a more intense sense of the reality of God or a more humbling sense of His grandeur than the late Dr Martyn Lloyd-Jones and it is unspeakably sad that those who claim to be his most ardent admirers are now pleading for forms of worship he would have deplored. Our worship should correspond to the nature of the God who is among us. This does not mean remaining enslaved to 17th century liturgies, Victorian hymns, Vatican collars or archaic translations of the Psalter. Neither can it mean, however, lowering the worship of God to a level where it is scarcely distinguishable from a disco.

Sola fide

The second major area of tension between Reformed theology and Pentecostalism relates to the principle of *sola fide*. According to the theology of the Reformation sinners were justified *by faith alone*. There was no *plus* of personal merit or human achievement. At the point of acceptance with God the whole truth about a human being was that he was an ungodly man who trusted in Christ. He was *simul iustus ac peccator* (at one and the same time a sinner and a justified man). But beneath this there is something else. The sufficiency of faith does not lie in itself. Its efficacy, at least as seen in Reformed thought, lies in the fact that it unites us to Christ. It links us to *His* righteousness and keys us in to *His* power. *Sola fide* really means *Solus Christus* (Christ alone). *He* is everything: and he who has *Him* has everything.

It is at this that the Charismatic movement strikes its most dangerous blows: and this is why it is incompatible with Reformed theology. We have gone over this ground already (see pages 6-8) and there is no need to repeat it here. Roman Catholicism argued that to be in Christ was not enough for justification: there had to be a *plus*. Pentecostalism argues that to be in Christ is not enough for Spirit baptism: there has to be a *plus*. It is possible, so we are told, to be in Christ and yet not to be baptised, not to be filled and not to be sealed. It is possible to be in Christ and never to have received the promise of the Father.

In the abstract, both the Romanist and the Pentecostal positions with their respective doctrines of *plus* may be true. But neither is compatible with the theology of the Reformation. Nor, in our judgment, are they compatible with the theology of the New Testament. What we read there is that a man is complete in Christ (Col. 2: 10) and that he who has the Son has life (1 John 5: 12). That is the gospel. We come to the Saviour not as to some half-way house nor as to a point at which we begin some new and arduous religious quest (for the baptism of the Spirit). We come to Him because He says to us, 'Come! and I will give you *rest*.'